THE CRAZY QUILT

A Memoir About Mental Illness

THE CRAZY QUILT

A Memoir About Mental Illness

ELIZABETH CASPER ROLFS

ReadersMagnet, LLC

The Crazy Quilt.
Copyright © 2005, 2022 by *Elizabeth Casper Rolfs.*

Published in the United States of America.

Library of Congress Number: 2003099388
ISBN Paperback: 978-1-959165-30-9
ISBN eBook: 978-1-959165-31-6

All rights reserved. No part of this publication may be reproduced, stored in a retrieval system or transmitted in any way by any means, electronic, mechanical, photocopy, recording or otherwise without the prior permission of the author except as provided by USA copyright law.

The opinions expressed by the author are not necessarily those of ReadersMagnet, LLC.

ReadersMagnet, LLC
10620 Treena Street, Suite 230 | San Diego, California, 92131 USA
1.619.354.2643 | www.readersmagnet.com

Book design copyright © 2022 by ReadersMagnet, LLC. All rights reserved.

Cover design by Ericka Obando
Interior design by Daniel Lopez

I have a mental illness.

It is major depression, a mood disorder.

It is not my fault.

Major depression is a serious medical condition with mixes of biological and psychological causes and a variety of definable signs and symptoms.

Major depression is treatable.

Contents

Dedication ix
Acknowledgments xi
Introduction xiii

Chapter One: Beth 1
Chapter Two: Postpartum Depression 53
Chapter Three: Family Of Origin 69
Chapter Four: Liz 107
Chapter Five: The Illness, The Healing, The Help 192
Chapter Six: Quilting Pieces 212
Chapter Seven: More Quilting Pieces 235

Afterward 265

Resources 266

This book is dedicated to my mother
Elsa C. Rolfs

Dedication

Mom this part of my story is for you. It was always you whom I could pour out my heart to, no matter what my hurting was about. You listened, you cared, you comforted me and you helped me have the necessary hope to go on—so many times over. It was because of your love and support that I was able to.

Not only in the treasures of our relationship did I find strength, but in the many day to day ways that you helped me encircle my children with tender stability. They go on now as adults rich in the spirit of who you have been. Thank you, Mom. We could not have made it through those terribly tough times without you.

I know that the times in my life when I suffered the most devastating effects of my major depression were extremely painful for you. I remember stories you would tell me later: the visits we shared in the hospital, the daisies you sent me; you driving over in the middle of the night to stay with the children while I was taken to have my stomach pumped. What I heard were your deep feelings of sadness. There was so little you could do to help your own child, whom you had tried for so long to shield and protect.

I know too Mom, how different your own life could have been were there the help you so needed and deserved. If only in your sad and lonely childhood, rebellious youth, sentimental and desperately insecure twenties, you hadn't been ignored or adored because of your own parents' illnesses. If only having so many babies, being the romantic and loyal wife and Good Catholic had not been the norm at that time. If only your poetry and music, created in the middle of the night, had not had to be put aside as you took up your duties of the day. I wish your many fears could have been taken seriously within the healing relationship of good therapy. I wish your whole worn out body/mind could have found relief in rest and with the aid of appropriate medication.

I feel my own sadness in that there was so little done for you. I imagine that my own times of feeling strong and well again brought deep satisfaction and joy to your heart. In fact, I know they did. We shared the happiness I felt. I can appreciate even more deeply now the hope and sense of possibility that my gradual changes must have represented to you.

It is because of what you already know and because of what I wanted to tell you that I dedicate this story to you. As in our past, I am able to be so open with you. I have called on the spirit of our loving friendship as I risked telling the truth that this story required. It was with respect for and in appreciation of the strengths I saw in you that I knew I had what it took to enable me to stand strong. Thank you Mom.

Acknowledgments

First and foremost, I acknowledge the Spirit of Mystery, Magic and of Miracle that has guided me here. There were many, many times when I did not want to go on living because I did not know how to, with the extent of pain I was in. It is absolutely by the intervention of a Power Greater than I know, that I am alive today. I am most grateful that I am.

I was gifted with two teachers that have been primary influences in my emotional development and my gradually increasing ability to stand tall. They were surrogate parent models for me at crucial times in my therapy process. Thank you, Irene Sylvester, for being patient as I cautiously moved closer, for holding me and feeding me your love. You told me I was beautiful and I began to believe you. Thank you, Jerry Rousseau, for accepting all of me, for being a wise and gentle counsel, always available. In your presence I began to hold myself securely. I am most grateful to each of you for your hope and faith in me, for your dedication and commitment to me as we went the long way home.

To the others, family and friends, who are most dear to me (especially you my precious children, who were my lifeline) I appreciate every single effort of yours to offer me support and understanding. I am calling on your energy to help me continue in this writing of my story.

To the staff in emergency rooms, backs of ambulances, police squads, psychiatric wards of hospitals and follow up clinics, for any of you who went out of your way to show me compassion in the midst of my deepest turmoil, I appreciate your kindness. You gave yourself to me. Someone cared.

To those of you I've met, with whom I share this common bond of mental illness, both inside and on the outside, you have helped keep me moving on. Your honesty has inspired me; your humor has brought me back to life and your own vulnerability has helped me know that I was not alone. Thank you so much.

Now, to properly acknowledge those of you who have assisted me directly in the creation of this book...

Thank you, Liz Hopkins, for the expertise in proofing that you brought to this project and for the many hours that you spent objectively reading my first draft in order to give me my initial feedback. Thank you, Cookie Anderson, for listening to each new development of mine with appreciation, diligently tracking down information for building a biography and for help to me in proofing and making corrections. Thank you Toni Shaw, who supported this writing from early on and bestowed on me my first honorary Ph.D. for having the courage to live through and to write about my experiences with mental illness. I could not have brought this book to fruition without the encouragement of each of you.

Introduction

Because I have been living in the silence of shame about my mental illness for over four and a half decades, I have decided to tell my story. As I am learning what it feels like to be more truly alive and to become more honestly whom I am inside, I want to throw off the shackles of who I am not.

I am not anymore a woman who finds my fulfillment in filling the needs of others or who is willing to deny whole part of myself so that other people can be comfortable around me. I learned to do that from my first breaths and I have spent too many valuable years of my lifetime simply adapting to that role. It meant everything to me to be loved and accepted. I tried so hard to be what I thought I was "supposed to be" that I literally lost myself in the process. My own unmet needs, hurts and my anger that I turned inward against myself, slowly became heavy weights that dragged me down into major depression again and again.

In our society, being mentally ill is definitely not acceptable. As was the norm in my past, we learned quickly not to tell. As women, we realized labels like hysterical, neurotic, demanding and dependent stigmatized us further. As young women giving birth and as older women at mid-life, while hormone levels fluctuated rapidly, we too often were silenced. We went on, wondering what was wrong with us. We felt afraid. We felt utterly and totally alone. There were too few places and people to turn to for the understanding, information and assistance we so deserved and needed.

In spite of the fact that the term "mentally ill" itself is a loosely defined and confusing phrase that I do not like, I am using it to name this part of who I am. Because of the horrible stigma it has represented in the past, it is a challenge still, to think it and to say it. This is one of the reasons that I do. My recent experiences with both in and outpatient psychiatric treatment have shown me that mental health services are changing and becoming responsive in a respectable way. This gives me hope.

I know that there are other mid-life and elderly women who have gone through the whole dark "institutionalization" process of the system, as it was. These holding places were known as asylums and then later as sanitariums. Although much improved from the times of our grandmothers and those who suffered before them, our own experience of being locked up behind bars to be simply ignored or worse yet, used, threatened and shamed, was frightening and dehumanizing. It was enough to have our lives torn to shreds by the ravishing effects of mental illness without being further hurt by the very people we trusted to help us. It is especially for you who have also traveled this long, dark path here that I write this book. You are no longer alone. We have survived it.

These days as I begin to tell many of the old secrets I have kept hidden, I feel steadily whole and well. There has been time now to think and to feel, to pull out what I have been learning from this part of my life. I am coming to a gentle place of understanding and acceptance and I have the courage to define my own story. I am discovering myself here with an interesting mix of pride and humility. It is in this process of healing and in the spirit of celebration that I choose today to share myself with you.

Names have been changed to protect
the privacy of people in my story...

Chapter One

Beth

I remember being at Karen's house. I was drawn to her home because I knew it would be peaceful. The old-fashioned farmhouse was at the end of a long drive, tucked into pine trees and the softly rolling hills of the North Kettle Moraine area. As we got closer I could see the spire rising tall from Holy Hill. Driving up this winding road past trees in every shade of green, I could feel myself beginning to relax.

Somehow I knew my sister would know what to do. It had been so hard for weeks now, the new baby crying through the nights and no chance for me to sleep during the day. There were two other children to take care of, one just past her first birthday and her three year old "big" sister. My husband wasn't home a lot. His job kept him away during the day, but I always had the impression that he looked for things to be involved with at night, so he wouldn't have to help with the work of the children or relate to me.

I'd been crying more and more easily in these weeks after the baby. I stopped caring how I looked; there just wasn't time or the energy. The bill collectors started to call, even showed up at the door. Through the peephole one morning,

I saw two men standing there in suits with briefcases. They were insistent; knew I was there. I felt as if I were being caught in a trap with all the pressures of my world caving in on me. That afternoon while the children slept, I climbed up on the kitchen counter and disconnected the doorbell. I really needed to protect myself from anymore stress coming in from the outside.

My sister Karen had always been my best friend, especially after Dad's death when I had just turned fifteen. She allowed me to come to her with my sadness, my fears, my discovery of boy friends and my frustrations with Mom. I knew I could trust her even in this, my most desolate moment. I drove up in the old green Chevy; me and my babies, their car toys, pacifiers, bottles, diapers and special blankets.

She greeted us in the near noon sunshine, surprised to see me, but warm and welcoming. She and I threw an impromptu lunch together while the children played. Then all of us gathered around the old kitchen table; our four with miniature glasses of milk in front of them, my sister and me with mugs of fresh coffee and my little one, content in his infant seat by my side. Karen left the kitchen for awhile, to answer a phone call or help one of her children with something. The next thing I remember, I was under the table. I had my baby with me, my arms around my girls and I huddled them tightly to me. I felt a tremendous need to be in this small, safe space. I needed to hide. I didn't ever, ever want to have to go back home.

Later that night I sat in his office with the big mahogany desk and bookcases all around. We had come into St. Mary's Hill Psychiatric Hospital earlier that evening. The quiet lobby was open, spacious, with green slip covered sofas and softly lit lamps on tables. The nuns there were the same order as at Grandpa's hospital, St. Mary's on Lake Drive and there was comfort in the familiarity. Father Reed had said I should be brought here when Karen called him in the afternoon.

I didn't know what to expect. I felt scared. Dr. Trayer was gentle, easy to talk to. Something about him felt familiar too; his thinness, slight stoop, white shirt and tie, crew cut, glasses. He talked with me for a long time it seemed and I was glad that someone was taking an interest in me. I began to feel relieved in being able to tell about myself and what I'd been going through in these last couple of months. Dr. Trayer asked questions, took notes, talked with my husband and suggested that I be admitted.

There must have been papers to sign, a telephone call to Mom who was home with the children. It's all very vague to me. I remember only feeling tremendously relieved that I could stay, that now someone was going to take care of me, like my sister had said. I wouldn't have to keep pushing myself anymore. I was feeling so worn out and so very alone.

* * *

That was my introduction to mental illness. It was the beginning of a long line of psychiatrists/psychologists/psychiatric institutions and the doctors and nurses who staffed them. It was the beginning of having labels put on me, so others would know what to do. It was the beginning of psychiatric "restraints," both in the form of tranquilizing medication (for the control of "psychotic symptomology" it said in my chart) and in the form of white, fabric "straight jackets" with long ribbon-like ties. It was the beginning of locked wards, windows that were barred and worse, the "isolation room" with it's padded walls. My first diagnosis was: "schizophrenic reaction; acute undifferentiated type." Prognosis was "guarded." I was twenty-three years old.

* * *

From the long window hung cream colored drapes that matched the bedspreads perfectly. I think there was carpeting on the floor, probably tan. There were old-fashioned brown metal beds; mine in the corner near the door of this small, two patient room. There was a dark wooden dresser, a framed mirror above it and in the corner near the window a small, tan upholstered chair with wooden arms. My room was right next to the nurses' station and at night I could hear soft voices speaking in friendly tones and it comforted me.

The next day I gradually made my way down the long hallway to the sun porch at the end. This was the only place where we are allowed to smoke and I was very uncomfortable having to sit with other patients that I didn't know, in order to have a cigarette. There would be small talk there, usually generated by one of the nun/nurses supervising us. Often there were long silences. I pretended to page through magazines or look out of windows in order to avoid the curious stares.

I much preferred time alone in my little room. There were days and nights when I felt especially fragile and I'd hide under my bed. I felt safe in my dark, warm cocoon; the soft wrapper of beige fabric enclosing me. Sometimes my special staff friend, Sister Mary Douglas, would kneel down on the floor to lift the fabric up a bit and talk to me. She never scolded or told me that I had to come out. She said, simply, that she was there to be with me so I wouldn't have to be all-alone.

There were frequent trips down to Dr. Trayer's office, where I began to open up and tell about some of the hurting places in my life. I hadn't done this with anyone before (well, maybe Karen and my best friend Serena from high school) yet it began to get easier each time, because I could feel that he really cared about me. It was like a lifeline to grab onto just as I was about to go under. In his careful attention to me and consistent orders for my care (he was not only my psychiatrist but the director of the whole hospital) I began to believe that maybe something about me was "worth it." Slowly, some spark of faith in my own value was being rekindled.

Relieved as I was to be away from home, with all of the demands of my household and marriage, I felt terribly worried about the impact my absence was having on my children. My oldest was taken into my sister Sally's family where already there were seven children, but I knew she'd be given lots of love and good solid care there. I wrote notes to her saying "Mommy loves you" and "Sometime soon we are all going to be back home together". My toddler was with Mom, whose home she was familiar with and probably having her crib there too was comforting. Her Grandpa was kind, played with her easily. Yet how do you reassure a toddler that Mommy really is coming back? His other Grandma, my mother-in-law, took my baby, just an infant, home to Ohio. It was decided that he would get the most consistent care there with both grandparents and a loving extended family. It was a place where he could stay for as long as was needed, too.

But I had been taking care of him since he was born. I had protected him, fed him, changed him, and rocked him, given up my sleep to help him get his. Now how would he be? I felt the deep wrenching pain of suddenly having my baby ripped away from me. I felt so unable to help all three of my children. This was the worst part about being in the hospital. Daily, I prayed for their innocent little hearts and minds that they would feel love encircling them and be protected in all of their fears. It was the only thing left that I was able to do for them. I discovered that this time in prayer also had a calming, healing effect in me.

* * *

I remember the hospitals' occupational therapy room, way up in a corner of the top floor. There were bay windows all around and as I stood looking out and down, I felt as though I were tucked safely into the turret of a castle. I learn how to knit there. I carefully make squares of green, brown, orange and yellow rows of stitches, evenly spaced, not too taught, orderly. Later I fitted them together into what I affectionately called my "crazy quilt." I stitched a sampler for my mom, blue stitches on a white background. It read "God I can push the grass apart and lay my fingers on thy heart." I had never been taught to do anything like this before and I loved it. It was soothing to me.

St. Mary's Hill hospital was just what I needed it to be. Physically, it was a beautiful, old, brick building that took up a good half of a city block. Outside, the corner was fenced with high, black rod iron; the kind of fence with spear headed posts that look regal and protective. There was a little patch of yard along the north side, with big trees (that later, I discovered, also circled around to include a backyard). Inside there were long hallways and dark, heavy wooden doors and wide, low windowsills with seats built right into them. There were gray/white marble fireplaces, octagon tiled floors and wide old, stone staircases. It was the kind of place that felt solid and stable to me and since I hadn't had that in my life, I welcomed the comfort it brought to me.

Here, I was being "taken care of." The real needs that I had: for uninterrupted sleep, for proper nutrition (I weighed only 107 lbs.), for physical rest and relaxation, for a sense of my own space, for quiet, all were being met. But more than that, the hustle and bustle of maternal energy, the nurses and nuns who were warmly present at all times, both capable and nurturing, helped fill a tremendous void in my soul. I felt the "presence of God" in these hallways and hearts. It touched me deeply and helped make me well.

Three times, in the course of about nine months, I went home and then came back into the hospital. At the time of my second admission, records show that I was seen as an outpatient, for a sodium amytal interview: "given to check on the nature of her underlying drives and impulse control." It showed that "self-destructive urges and urges against her children were felt to be quite prominent and evidence indicated weakened impulse control." I was re-admitted on an emergency basis by Dr. Trayer.

By my third admission, hospital notes read: "Since last hospitalization, patient has repressed her impulses to harm her children, but remains quite depressed, with the depressive symptomology getting progressively worse. At the time of admission, the patient is quite hopeless and pessimistic but is showing more affect than she had heretofore and this time asked for the admission and help. She will be considered for electroshock therapy."

This part of my hospitalization was hard for me. I remember feeling guilty enough, that I'd had some fears about hurting my children, but now on top of it, I was going to be leaving them again. I was worried about what this was going to do to them emotionally. They were so little and there was no way they could begin to understand.

My oldest was told that Mommy was sick, she was in the hospital and that she'd get better and be home soon. I didn't think that at four years old she could really grasp the concept of me coming back and she must have felt so betrayed. Hospital notes say that she refused to talk with her father when he went to my sister's to visit with her and that she often acted angry with him. The two little ones knew only that neither parent was there, that their world revolved around Grandma (and thank God both Grandmas were patient and loving, in spite of being over-extended in energy). Not one of us could have made it through this horrendous crisis without both of them.

The shock treatments started. I did not understand what they were, or how they would be given or in what way they were supposed to work. I just knew that I did not have a choice about it, that I had to have them. The whole ordeal really frightened me.

It was in my bedroom, in my bed, that the treatments would be given to me. Something about that seemed strange, maybe because now my only real "safe space" wasn't safe anymore. It was always early in the morning. Dr. Trayer would come in, in his white shirt and tie, and I'd be embarrassed that he'd see me in my nightgown.

Then pushed through the doorway would be a cart on wheels, with a wooden boxlike machine on it that had lots of black wires attached to it. The nurse would help me turn around in bed, so my head would be at the foot and the cart with the machine would be positioned next to my head. They tucked my pillow under my shoulders and put a sandbag under the back of my neck and another heavy one across the top of my ankles and feet. Then the wide, leather strap with the buckle got wrapped around the top of my head, and that big, black, rubber thing was put in mouth.

I always felt really, really scared right then, because I didn't know what was going to happen next. Dr. Trayer would be sitting on a chair next to me and the nurse would be standing behind my head. Then I'd get a shot in my right arm. That was all I ever remembered. I'd wake up later in the day, always confused and I'd have an awful, awful headache for hours afterward.

Years later my mom told me how hard it was for her to consent to the stock treatments. She said that she and my husband had been called in to talk with Dr. Taheyr. He had explained that it was a treatment of last resort and the only thing he knew to suggest, that might jolt me out of the catatonic state I was in. He told them that without trying it, I may never regain my ability to be cognizant of who or where I was, or regain my ability to communicate again. In that case, I may have to be institutionalized for the rest of my life.

Many, many years later my husband with tears in his eyes, was to tell our middle child that signing that consent form was the hardest thing he ever had to do. According to hospital records, I went through a series of 20 shock treatments, within a three-month period of time. In view of all the controversy now surrounding the practice of ECT (electric convulsive therapy) I have to say that to this day, I believe the three people who were responsible for me and the decisions affecting me at that time, made the right choice.

There were other things that made being in the hospital very hard. Dr. Trayer had come to believe that the root of my depression lay in delayed grief over the sudden death of my father (by now, nine years earlier). He realized the heavy inhibitions I had about allowing myself to be angry (part of the "good girl" script/my Catholic, guilt laden upbringing) and knew it would take more than "talking therapy" to help me move through them. So he ordered me to be locked in my room and simply told to "get angry."

It made absolutely no sense to me whatsoever. I sat on my bed and tried to figure it out. I had to ask permission to go to the bathroom. My meals were brought in on a tray. I think it was about the third day that I absolutely couldn't stand it anymore. Suddenly, I threw all my things on the floor/yelled and screamed obscenities/pulled the long, beige draperies down from the window and picked up my chair and smashed it into the mirror over my dresser. It felt absolutely exhilarating.

I have no idea how long I acted that anger out. I do remember the nuns unlocking my door and rushing in to protect and to congratulate me. By this point I was totally exhausted. Though not real clear why, I did know that my ability to be angry was a good thing. It had shocked me to feel such an extent of rage cursing through my whole body. For the first time ever, I experienced this anger as an important and powerful part of who I was as a person.

I wanted to go home. I missed my children, my home itself, and my other life. When I asked if I could go, I was told no, I "wasn't well enough yet to get a pass." It didn't seem right to me that they could make me stay, even if I didn't want to be there, so I left anyway. I gathered up my soda machine change for the bus, pretended I was going to be in the yard and simply walked right out of the black Iron Gate.

Walking as far out of the neighborhood, as quickly as I could, I never dared to look back to see if I was being followed. I would find my way home. I remember trying to sound casual, as I asked the bus driver where to make the connections. I felt smug, because I was pulling it off.

Somehow I got into my house, though it had never occurred to me how to do that without my key. I have a vague memory of going to the apartment complex office (luckily on the property) and picking up a spare. I was so happy to be home. Immediately I went upstairs and looked into my children's rooms, almost expecting to find them. It comforted me just to see their waiting beds. I grabbed a pillow and blanket, went back down to lock the front and back doors, pulled shades down and contentedly snuggled into the couch and went to sleep.

The next thing I knew, three big policemen were standing in my living room. The hospital had reported me missing and given my address to them. When I didn't answer the doorbell (after they had seen me on the couch, by looking around the edges of the shades) they banged down the door. They said they were afraid I had tried to kill myself. I felt so frustrated by having been found, confused by their questions, intimidated by their size, numbers and uniforms. I was so angry I had to go back, was being taken forcibly right out of my home. I was scared. I had never done anything like this before and I didn't know what the consequences would be.

The Crazy Quilt

There was another afternoon that stays with me. Out in the little patch of grass in the side yard of the hospital, I grappled with the despair inside me against the back drop of what was so serene all around me, wanted so much, to find some relief from this pain. Watching a gray squirrel run down the side of a tree and across the yard, I thought that maybe, if I crouched down into the grass and concentrated on disappearing, that God would take me right into the earth and I'd finally be gone. I stayed there, curled up into a still form against the ground, for a long time. Nothing more happened. I got up and walked very, very slowly back into die building.

* * *

At the time of my discharge from St. Mary's' Hill, according to hospital records, I "showed considerable memory defect as a result of the shock treatments and was somewhat distant and apathetic. It was felt at this time that this was the best possible adjustment in view of the severity of her illness". Dr. Trayer and staff advised my family to continue my hospitalization, but I was needed back home to resume the care of the children, so I was discharged. I was told to follow up as an outpatient; with continued medication and supportive therapy. It was decided that "no attempt will be made at insight therapy until and unless she shows some stability and remission of her schizophrenic symptoms."

I was not ready to go home and that became apparent during the subsequent hospitalizations. It was noted that my husband "as previously, showed a lack of insight into the severity and significance of his wife's illness and we have made attempts to involve him in collateral therapy with the social service department." Looking back, I see how easy it was for him to abdicate his responsibility in this marriage to me and how I naturally assumed it, believing of course that the heart of our problem was my fault. I believed, basically, that I wasn't okay as a person, much less as a wife. My pattern would be that I'd build new resolve to "try harder," find after a while that my efforts did nothing but exhaust me, feel like a failure and shame myself terribly, then want to give up completely. When I left the hospital I did not want to go back home, to the loneliness of our relationship. The only thing that I wanted was knowing soon that I would hold my precious children in my arms.

I was discharged with a 10 day supply of valium, 5 mg. qid/ sparine, 50 mg. qid/ hygroton, 100 mg. 2 tablets daily/ pyribenzamine, 25mg. at 10:00 PM and seconal, gr. 1 1/2 Hs.—My final diagnosis was "schizophrenic reaction, schizo-affective type." Results of treatment were that I had improved, was "in partial, brittle remission" and that "prognosis is guarded." It was 1967.

* * *

I knew nothing about mental illness at this stage of my life, leading me to believe of course that how I felt and the problems that I was having were totally the product of my own incompetence as a person. I had been diagnosed as schizophrenic, which later bothered me because it didn't seem an accurate description of what I was going through. Since then, I've come to understand that it was my behavior at the time that was schizophrenic (in reaction to the internal/external stresses I experienced) rather than me having the disorder of "schizophrenia." A more true diagnosis would have been that I had "an affective disorder," one of the major mental illnesses that are disorders of mood.

Affective disorders refer to severe depression (my disease) and bipolar depression (characterized by alternating cycles of depression and mania or excitement). "Unlike the normal down mood that we all experience at one time or another, major depression drags on and becomes more pronounced than warranted by the normal ups and downs of daily living. During a major depressive episode, a person looses interest in almost all activities, experiences feelings of hopelessness and worthlessness, has thoughts of death and dying and may exhibit suicidal behavior."

Following my final release from St. Mary's Hill hospital (known to St. Mary's "family" affectionately as "The Hill"), I continued to feel totally incapable and in addition, now I was alone. At first it was exhilarating to be home, to be in my own surroundings. I'd had my freedom restored to me; I could come and go as I wished, make choices about what kind of food I wanted for supper, decide what time I wanted to go to bed. These simple things, I found so precious to have within the realm of my control again. Slowly, I began to feel like I was coming back to life. Out patient therapy with Dr. Trayer was supportive and my husband took me in for evening appointments, at first.

The children came home, all three of them and I was especially grateful to be able to hold my baby in my arms; to feed him, to comfort him, to lay him down to sleep. We had been separated from each other so suddenly, so soon. My toddler had grown taller, was putting words together in ways I hadn't heard before. She seemed cautious around me.

Luckily her rapport with her dad had been unbroken and that helped her make the transition back home. I held her on my lap and we looked at books, slowly feeling close again. My oldest daughter was the easiest to welcome home. It helped that we could talk together, play "remember when" about some of her favorite activities and toys. We had established certain routines that now we could go back to, for the comfort of familiarity.

By the time the children were home again full time and I had gradually picked up pieces of my old homemaker role; doing grocery shopping/cooking/laundry/ cleaning etc. I was exhausted. It was too much, too fast. I was without any substantial help from my already overextended family and I did not have friends in my life to offer understanding, caring and actual hands-on help.

By now, I found there was a gapping emptiness in my relationship with my husband. He knew only to react (his part of this "family" crisis) by running away, physically and emotionally. I had the tendency to turn things inward, feeling "to blame" for everyone else's unhappiness and believing that my inadequacies were responsible for my husband's behavior. When he was away, which became the "norm," I simply did everything that had to be done, by myself, and did it to the best of my ability. When eventually he did come home (and I never knew when that was going to be), a bitter silence hung heavily in the space between us. I was too angry and too hopeless that anything could ever really change, to even express my anger.

It was a night like that, after many, many nights like that, when I made my first suicide attempt. I had been feeling myself going down, down, down. I knew, for maybe a day or two before hand, that the best way out of this constant pain was to be dead. I hadn't been sleeping or eating regularly again, and the headaches were coming back. After taking care of the children's needs, I had absolutely no energy left to take care of mine. In fact, even to allow myself to have needs and to decipher what they were was totally beyond my experience.

Secretly I was even beginning to doubt my ability to be good mother; something that before had always come so naturally to me. I was shocked at myself, when one morning I had an impulse to suddenly push my oldest daughter down the basement steps. It was laundry day and she was standing in front of me at the top of the stairs; I was frustrated that she wasn't moving fast enough when I had two other kids calling and so much to do. She was only four years old, vulnerable and innocent. I never actually touched her, it was only a flashing thought, but it absolutely horrified me. Now I wasn't even sure if I could trust myself not to hurt my own children.

As in the past, I was crying often and in my tears, feeling so without control over anything at all. I felt separated from everyone, especially my husband who was so unwilling or unable to show me concern, compassion, friendship or love. I felt nothing but being totally drained, empty and the hollow hurting of being so very lonely.

That last day, I put things in order; vacuumed and dusted, stacked nice clean diapers up on the dresser. Before dinner I gave my little ones their baths and put them in soft, sweet smelling pajamas. There was always a feeling of accomplishment, of peacefulness in me after a day like that. On this night I almost felt happy, relieved maybe, that soon my job would be over. We ate dinner. I did the dishes while my husband played with the children in the living room and watched TV. I came and got them one by one, slowly put them into their beds, tucked the covers in, bent over and gave each one a long, last kiss on their forehead. Then

I forced myself to ease away, step by step, silently saying good-bye.

My husband was engrossed in his "shoot'em up" westerns on TV. I knew he wouldn't even wonder where I was for several more hours. Knowing that hurt deeply. It confirmed, all the more for me, that this was the only way out of the pain.

I locked the bathroom door, drew hot water into the tub for a bath, undressed and dimmed the light. I looked at myself for a long, long time in the mirror. I think I was wondering who I really was, looking for some spark of recognition, wanting to see someone I knew, someone that I could stay alive for. There was no one familiar there, no answers. It didn't surprise me. It was what I had come to expect.

Swallowing down all my pills was easier than I thought it would be. Five handfuls; blue, shiny red capsules, small white tablets, lavender, yellow. I did it quickly. I stood and looked in the mirror again, "There, it's done." Finally reclaiming, in the only way left now, my sense of power. I bent and stepped into the hot, soothing tub, lay my head back against the cool porcelain and took deep, calming breaths. I waited. I waited and waited. Nothing was happening. I was not being taken away. Where was the relief that I so desperately needed? I felt angry, thinking, "Damn, I had planned every detail of this so well." After a long while, I gave up, got out and clumsily began to dry. Then I remember sinking slowly, slowly to the floor, feeling tremendously relieved.

Two days later I woke up in a strange bed. They told me it was a hospital. I couldn't imagine why I was there or how I had gotten there. Strangers were saying things like;

"You're okay—it's okay now," but I wasn't okay—I wanted to be dead. These people, this place, it meant nothing to me. I did not want to be there.

Mom told me later how my husband had found me that night, out cold on the bathroom floor (had I unlocked the door on my way down?) He was really scared, she said, didn't know what was wrong, carried and laid me onto our bed, called her. It was late but she came right over to stay with the children while he and a neighbor put me into the car and drove to the nearest emergency room. I was throwing up, she later told me and hospital staff continued to empty my stomach and to observe me until I stabilized. She said I slept for almost two days. Said everyone in the family was worried about and praying for me.

I did not want their worry or their prayers. No one in my family really knew me (except Mom), or knew what I was going through. Even if I believed they cared, I couldn't have put it into words to tell them, couldn't explain even to myself. I had long ago lost hope in the one person in the world, who I did want to care about me, respond to me as if he could.

There was a phone at my bed side and I called my sister Sally, asked her to tell me what was going on. The nurses were talking about discharging me in a day or so. I couldn't stand it! I couldn't leave here! I couldn't go back where I came from! I couldn't balance on this precarious edge any longer.

In desperation I lowered the rails on my bed and rolled very deliberately over the side, so that I fell flat. I remember hearing the loud "thud," feeling how cold the hospital floor was. When I "came to" again, I was tied down and that scared me. My wrists were tied to the side rails by long, ribbon like streamers and my ankles were tied somehow too. My head was hurting a lot. They told me that I had fallen out of bed. (No one ever knew.) They said that I was being transferred to the psychiatric ward. It had worked. I was glad.

I wandered the halls in the psyche ward at St. Michael's' Hospital. There were long halls and I had the freedom to walk them as I wanted to. Occasionally I had a therapy session with a young, naive doctor. It didn't really help much, but it had bought me some time. At the end of two weeks, I went home reluctantly. I was glad to be with my children again, but overwhelmed with loneliness and the beginning of sad grieving over what I knew now, was my lost marriage.

When there was an opening in my husband's family trade for an apprentice to begin working alongside his Dad and Uncle, he wanted to apply and move back to his hometown in Ohio. There was never any question about me and the children coming along, it was simply assumed that we would. I wanted to believe that the change could be good for us as a family. So, against the medical advice of my original psychiatrist, who I was still seeing (he had said I was not yet stable enough for such a big change), I moved with my children and husband, back to his small town. Tucked into the foothills of the mountains, where I had come before as a young wife and mother, I started out again to begin a new life.

I had no real sense of myself as a person suffering through a major depression and in need of ongoing medical treatment, psychotherapy and/or medication. I made the assumption that what I'd been through in the past was related only to disappointments in my marriage and my exhaustion;

taking full time care of three children under the age of four. I did not know how to evaluate my life as "separate," as an individual in my own right, outside of the roles of "mother/ wife/ daughter/ sister/ aunt." I was completely ignorant of the fact that I had my own, legitimate, wants and needs— much less my own responsibility to recognize those needs and to fulfill them.

What I did know at that point in my life (I was 25-26) was that my job was to make a comfortable home for my husband and children and to give as much love to each of them as I possibly could. I knew that if I gave, to the best of my ability, God would help me find happiness in my family and be satisfied in my intense longing for His love of me. Church was an important part of my life, always had been. I found comfort in prayer, in the Sunday ritual, in communion and the quiet time and the singing. I asked for God's help. I tried so hard, to please Him.

My husband's family welcomed us back once more and we settled into a big, old, white house on a quiet, tree lined street in town. A miracle hapened, in that I found a friend. Ellen was my first real friend since Julie (across the hall in the navy town, at the start of my marriage). I knew in those early days that something important was missing in my marriage, and my friendship with Julie helped me to fill that gap. Now I had Ellen, who understood when I tried to talk about things close to my heart. Ellen and I had challenging conversations about ideas (it was at the beginning of some feminist consciousness, in both of us) and her friendship with me eased some of the pain of my loneliness.

My husband had made it into the training program, (in the family trade) and he attended classes several nights a week with his Dad and brother, out of town. Soon the other nights that he had been home were traded in for time on a bowling league and at the pool hall. After a while the words he said to me were "I'm going down to get some Oreos (sometimes it was bologna)" but really the unspoken message was "I'll be gone for a few days and nights." He'd come home after several days, change clothes, play with the kids and leave again. I never asked him where he had been.

I took care of the children, did the laundry, cleaned the house, made the meals, grocery shopped and visited with his Mom and Dad. They often had me and the children over for supper, and would just show up at the door late in the afternoon saying they came to bring me to their house. The children would be waking up from their naps and I would be dreading the loneliness of mealtime and an evening without another adult by my side. The wisdom and willingness of this family to take us in and give us their love nurtured the children and me and kept us going from day to day.

I really don't remember quite how this came about, but I ended up back in the hospital again. I think it was connected to the time that I was on my way to the basement to do laundry. When I turned the light on and looked down, it seemed like the basement floor was swaying and moving in waves. Watching in horror, I soon realized that the entire floor of the wet basement, built into a hill, was swarming with big, brown water bugs. It was absolutely a shocking, ugly, terrifying experience.

It sent me reeling through the wall of denial I had been hiding behind. I was shocked to realize how ugly the neglect was in my marriage (which I hadn't visited in truth, just as I hadn't visited the basement, in a long while). Neighbors had recently told me what they said the whole small town knew. They had tried to protect me but realized it was better to tell. The man I was married to was having affairs with two other women, managing to live with one of them, part time. That was it! My experience of excruciating emotional pain about the failure of my marriage was horrendous.

* * *

This time the hospital was not the gracious, old, private sanitarium with the black rod iron fences and the well-tended gardens. It was not the modern psychiatric ward in the new medical building with an emergency room that was well equipped to pump stomachs, either. This time it was "out at the State Hospital" and everybody in town knew what that place was like. It was a huge complex of brown, brick buildings like barracks, safely far away from town, where the most severe, long-term mental illness cases (the insane) and all of the poor people go.

I don't remember how I got there, what the admission process was like or who was with me. I think I was transferred from some intake ward, to this prison-like "back alley" where no one came in and no one went out, except the big, fat matrons with loud voices and big, round circles of jangling keys. I didn't know anything about where I was or even why I was there. I just knew that it was a place I felt very afraid of and a place that I thought I would most likely never get out of.

I remember being issued a housedress and socks and underwear pants that were way too big, a bra and some slippers. I have always hated big, stiff, brown slippers like that. They slapped against the concrete floor when I walked. I remember that I had to wash the floor in the dorm, where I slept (it was just another section of the one big room where we all stayed, sort of an L shaped room, with old iron beds in three or four rows along the hall like space at the short part of the L). Someone brought me a big bucket on wheels and I was embarrassed to say I didn't know how to ring out the rag mop, so I ended up with a lot of cold, soapy water splashing on my bare legs. Washing the floor became my regular job. It was scheduled for 8:00 o'clock in the morning.

When we went to have breakfast, we walked very slowly in a long, long line through underground tunnels. The tunnels connected all the buildings, so we never had to put jackets on or go outside. We ended up in a big cafeteria and after filing through the food line we sat together at long tables to eat oatmeal or scrambled eggs. We were not allowed to talk to each other. That was okay with me, because I was pretty scared of everybody anyway, especially any of the matrons in case I made a mistake and broke one of the rules. So, I just kept quiet and watched everything, trying to figure it out.

There was one part of the day that I liked and even looked forward to. It was our time to be with each other, in the afternoon. By then I had found another mother there and we'd talk, and talk about our children. She had a split in one of her pierced earlobes and told me that her little boy, when he was a baby, had reached up and pulled at one of her hoop earrings. It tore through her ear lobe. I thought about how that must have hurt and in that, began to realize that I wasn't all-alone anymore. I was grateful to her, for being so real to me and for someone else who knew what it was like to be separated from her children. We'd all sit in a circle around the big pot of hot water they'd brought in on a cart with squeaky wheels. The instant coffee tasted terrible, but it was part of what we shared when we were just being ourselves and that made it wonderful to me.

Mom and Peter (her second husband) were in town taking care of the children I think. They came to visit once (it was my only visitation) and brought me a carton of cigarettes, Benson and Hedges gold, a compact with a mirror in it and my tennis shoes. Having my own shoes back was the best part. I remember that I felt very self conscious and uncomfortable, having to "visit" with Mom and Peter. I didn't know what to say and I was glad when they left, though I felt guilty about that.

It was soon after their visit that I was told I had an appointment with a psychiatrist in the out patient department. He was going to decide if I was ready to go home. The idea of going home was sudden and scary to me. I didn't know how I'd be able to take care of my children, much less do any of the housework. I just felt so totally drained of any confidence I'd ever had, any self-esteem or any ability.

This time, the hospitalization had really taken me down. There had been no therapy. There had been no support. There had been no help what so ever given to me. I was simply medicated (and looking back now, I'll bet heavily too) and warehoused in a situation where I had no access to anything to hurt myself with and where I was monitored 24 hours a day. My environment asked very little of me and gave very little back to me. I felt dull, small, weak, insignificant, and almost non-existent.

There was just one thing that I still cared about, and that was the state of my soul/my connection with God. Someone had told me, perhaps my sister-in-law Darlene, to ask to speak to the chaplain whose ministry there was to us, the mentally ill patients. I was surprised when my request was granted and I was allowed to walk unguarded, across the courtyard to his residence.

He saved my life that day we talked; he truly did. I risked revealing my unhappiness in my marriage and how torn I felt with the church admonishment against divorce. I talked about my children and how they needed me and yet I didn't know how I could go on with this kind of aching in my heart. I talked about how I wanted to be "good" and in God's graces. I talked and he listened. No one had really listened to me in a long, long time. He gave me his blessing and said, "You are a beautiful woman and you are going to be even more beautiful when you no longer have him in your life dragging you down." I was thrilled. Here was this chaplain, an "official" voice of the Catholic Church, giving me "permission" to get my husband out of my life. I had what I needed now to get well. I had the small beginnings of hope; I had the option of "choice" in my life and I had the desire to use it to begin to live.

I was released just a few days after this and began an outpatient process with my new therapist who was a psychologist. I must have continued on medication, because it was to be quite a long time before I had another relapse. My therapist was also a hypnotist and he began to work with me by trying out my suggestibility in a trance state. He was focused on my sexuality and I began to think that it might save my marriage for me to find some way to be sexually interested again. He had me read about cybernetics, which was becoming a popular therapeutic tool in the late 60's. I believe it was the work of Matthew Maltz and I was excited that Si (my therapist) thought that I could be sharp enough mentally to grasp the concepts. He said that I was an excellent hypnotic subject. We began to work together and this was the first time that I felt enthused about the therapeutic process. I thought that with Si's guidance I might really be able to make some changes in my life.

I tried at first to sexually experiment with my husband. For a while we worked together on this part of our relationship. Then my interest waned; I think I was just too angry and hurt by now to want to open up with him in any way physically or spiritually. I asked for a separation shortly after this. The chaplain had helped me know that I deserved to have a life and my work with Si had begun to show me how to go about creating the kind of life I wanted. I filed papers for a legal separation knowing that it would most likely lead to a divorce. I knew then, that I did not want this man to be living with me; being gone 3/4 of the week and me at home with the children, wondering if and when he was going to come back.

It was about two months after the seperation that one night, totally distraught over the crisis situation I was having with my children, I placed an emergency call to Si asking for help. My middle child who slept in her crib in the same room with the baby, wouldn't stop crying. I had tried everything: burping her, changing her, feeding her, rocking her. She screamed in that high pitched, frantic sound—keeping the other two awake until I couldn't stand it anymore. The next thing I knew I was standing over the headboard of her bed with a hammer in my hand, ready to raise my arms and swing to hit her in the head. I just wanted her to stop crying. I gasped in shock as I caught myself, ran down the steps and put in an emergency call to Si. Panicked, I begged him to help me and said I was afraid to be left alone with my children. To keep away from this precious baby of mine, I made myself lie down on the kitchen floor and told myself to stay there until help showed up. I just sobbed. I felt so guilty, so full of rage, so bad. I was so scared.

A short time later Si arrived with his wife (thinking I might have to be hospitalized and she could stay with the children while he admitted me). The children had all fallen asleep by now. The three of us talked and it calmed me. He sent his wife home saying he would just stay a while to make sure I was all right. He put his arm around me as we sat on the couch and I cried. He comforted me. Then he kissed me. Then he touched my breast. Then he laid on top of me. Then he raped me.—When he left I remember locking the door very carefully, yet I knew there was no place that was safe for me now, not even my own living room. As I lay in my bed in the dark that night, I felt utterly and totally empty and alone.

I divorced my husband. In those days you had to have a reason. My reason was mental cruelty. In court I testified to seven years of loneliness, my worn hopes and dreams. I talked about my "nervous breakdown," my time spent on psychiatric wards, the affairs my husband had. (I'd seen one of the women he was involved with the week before when he came to say good-bye to the children. The two of them had just showed up, started playing with the children in the back yard and given them each stuffed bunnies for Easter gifts. I was furious).

These days I was starting to feel my anger more. I had been through so damn much and missed out on experiencing so many other things. Life was hard and I was starting to feel hard, closed up inside and with the beginning of a protective edge around me. It had occurred to me, somewhere along the way, that the failure of my marriage was not all my failing and my fault. It was new to see that some of the important others in my life had been irresponsible, had let me down by their own failing, had hurt me by their own choices, had betrayed me by their own denial. The sadness that I had known all of my life was turning into anger. I felt strengthened by it and relieved.

* * *

I came back here to Milwaukee after my divorce, with my three children and two suitcases. I had nothing else. I had no money. I had no new dreams. I had to build a life for myself and my children and somehow soothe us through the jarring losses we had suffered. I had to make a new home for us. I had to make a new beginning. There was one thing going for me and I latched onto it with all of my energy: I had a sense of "possibility." The way was clear now, to develop my life on my terms. I was free to love and nurture and build with my children without any gnawing sense of disappointment or hurt, because of depending on a husband, or a traditional sense of family for my happiness.

My mom and my sisters helped tremendously. They welcomed us home and provided us with so much assistance. My mom had recently inherited some money from her mothers' estate and bought a townhouse in a small suburban community, for us to live in, so that I could be near my sister Sally and the shelter of her family. They brought over trucks and clothes for the children and blocks and blankets. They invited us over for meals. My other sisters wrote letters/ gave me encouragement and sometimes helped me laugh at myself. They were interested in my being well and they wanted to help me with my children. I felt loved.

Finally, I was on the road to respecting myself. I wanted to try to "put together" the pieces of my past, especially the times of deep depression/the suicide attempts/the hospitalizations. My Mom referred to those times as when I was "sick." That always bothered me because I wasn't sick, as in "mentally ill," I told myself. I wasn't "crazy;" I didn't imagine things or hear voices. I was just plain and simply depressed. But I was free from my marriage now and I wanted to go into therapy to work out the rest of it and learn how to make my own future.

I called Dr. Trayer, the man who had been my psychiatrist and was director of the private psychiatric hospital I had been in when this started. He was listed in the book at a new address and I made an appointment through his wife who was being his part time secretary. I knew that Dr. Trayer had cared about me and I trusted that he could help me integrate this stuff from the past and adjust to this role as a divorcee and single Mom. I hoped for a little while he could put me back on medication until I could stabilize, especially so I could sleep.

I tracked him down, now in his own private practice and I felt excited and scared to see him again. It had been two years. I wanted him to see me being "well," being "in charge" of my life! In some ways, he had always seemed like a "father" to me even though he was only 15 years older. Maybe it was because he looked like my Dad: crew cut, glasses, always white shirt and tie. Maybe it was because my Dad had died just after I turned fifteen (was starting to date) and the gaping hole inside hurt a lot because I missed him. Or maybe it was because Dr. Trayer had really "taken care of me" like I'd wanted at least one of my parents to. During my first hospitalization, he had spent hours listening to me, asking questions, offering direction, ordering tests and medication and special nursing care, sitting by my bedside during treatments, having me come back to work with him after being discharged, advising me not to make the changes to move out of town. I wanted to come back to him, ask for his help again and to show him how good I was doing. I wanted him to be proud of me.

In our first few sessions, I told him about being sexually exploited (though I didn't know the word then) by my old psychologist Si. I wanted to relieve my guilt and shame, to talk about my sadness and anger. I don't remember ever getting to the "exploring my feelings" part. Within the first month back, Dr. Trayer was telling me to call him George and asking me to sit on his lap. Within the second month we were focused on my problem of "ambivalence" (another word I didn't understand back then, I had to go home and look it up) toward him and about his suggestion. I began then, talking about my father. By the third month we were drinking together (my office visits now at night and lasting 3 to 6 hours) and dancing to slow songs on the radio. I was listening to his problems now. He was telling me about his marriage that wasn't working, the inevitability of divorce and about his feelings in relationship to his children. He told me that he loved me.

Naturally by this time, George and I were being sexual. This, I assumed, is just what happened when a man and a woman fell so madly "in love." I never even thought about refusing to please him. He used me like this, sexually and emotionally, for what seemed like a long time, but actually was only for about 6 months. I allowed him to. I believed he was in love with me. It was exciting and wonderful, the romance of the forbidden, the danger. He kept brandy for me in his office. He wrote prescriptions for me; mellerell/ elevil/ valium/ seconal/ demoral. We smoked cigarettes, talked, and cried, listened to music, danced, made love. He wanted me. Most of all he needed me. I felt high with it! Powerful!

I began to need him too and that was my downfall. I showed up at his house early one evening, needing emergency therapy. Another time, I rang his doorbell late at night and when he finally answered, yelling at me "No, not now." I felt hurt and confused. Still another time, I arrived at his office uninvited, very late at night and found him "in session" with somebody else. He suggested I lie down in the back room while waiting and gave me a shot to "help me relax." I didn't wake up until the next morning and staggered out, feeling humiliated, around 9:30 am, past office staff and his partner from "The Hill," tucking in my lavender silk blouse, adjusting my new brunette wig.

Then there was the time I desperately tried to slash my wrists in the women's room down the hall from his office, just before my appointment. I was trying to decide if I should "check myself in" to the hospital. He told me that if I did (my only option was now the old "County Hospital" where I wouldn't have to pay) he couldn't be my doctor because he was not on staff there. He did tell me though that he would come to visit.

So I admitted myself, went right from his office to the hospital. During those first long days and evenings, I waited for him. I waited, while lying on my stomach on my bed, listening for the promise of his footsteps coming down the long hall. I waited, while sitting in the orange plastic chair in the lounge, watching so I could see him coming in the locked door at the end of the hallway. Slowly, very slowly, I began to know that George was never going to come to see me, that he was never going to save me. I was devastated. I was shocked. I was angry. I was heart broken. I was sad. Months later from the safety of time and distance, I wrote a short and terse note to him at his office saying that I would never be back.

Reluctantly, on the advice of the discharge staff, I made an appointment with a psychiatrist they had recommended. After a few weeks, it seemed like he just couldn't grasp the emotional devastation I was feeling about having to end my previous relationship and really not wanting to. Dr. Parnell was expecting and encouraging me to be angry, to see that I had allowed myself to be used. He pointed out that I had, in fact, been prostituting myself without even getting paid for my services. I wasn't the least bit angry. I felt only sad, confused and lonely. In bitter frustration, I realized that he wouldn't be able to help me because he didn't understand me and by the third session I quit. More than 25 years later, I found and contacted Dr. Parnell by phone at his home. Yes, he'd had an office in that building during those years. To my delight and sense of validation, he said, "Oh I remember a Beth, kind of scared, shy and timid. You don't sound that way anymore." What a victorious moment that was for me. Yes, I had made it through and for many years now, I'd been living on the other side.

Wanting to get some help back then to work this through, I looked into my first therapy group. I remember finding the elite 400 East Whitefish Bay office complex and going through an interview with still another gray suited psychiatrist. He told me that the group members were other housewives, some in middle age, and that the fee was $50.00 once a week. I left terribly disappointed: it was way too expensive and my situation set me so far apart from the kind of women he was describing.

Next, I found out about a phone "hot line" called The Underground Switchboard. There was a suicide prevention phone line too, operated by Milwaukee County Mental Health Center. Both became a tremendous help to me at this point in my life. I could call from home, not have to arrange for childcare and I could call anytime. I did not have to identify myself. There were no judgments made against me. There was nothing that I had to commit to follow through on. So late at night, alone with my feelings, I found out that I could talk to someone who listened and seemed to care. I held onto the phone lines like they could save my life, and in fact they did. It became one of these links, Underground Switchboard, that led me to my first "rap group."

It was on Thursday nights in somebody's living room, near Oklahoma Avenue or Lincoln. There were a couple of Vietnam vets struggling with stress and flashbacks and the guilt of having survived when their buddies didn't. There were some people in the group with drug dependencies trying to break their habits. Then there was me, a young single mom with severe depression and thoughts of suicide. It was exciting to realize for the first time, that there were troubled others like me, living on the "outside" of the hospital wards. They had unmet needs too and were trying to move through them with each other's help. I learned about Carl Rogers and his active listening approach, reading everything I could about these new therapies cropping up at places like Esalan. I began to feel some stirrings of hope and to feel less totally identified by loss and shame.

After a while, I told my group about ending my therapy with Dr. Trayer and why I did. This led to the group facilitator, himself a psychiatrist (though still wearing the suit from the "other world", he had a relatability about him that I could trust) telling me during a break one night, that he thought he knew who it was I had been talking about. He'd heard of two other women recently with exactly the same story, and it sounded to him like the same therapist. He asked if I would mind telling him his name, so I swallowed, took a breath, risked it and did. It was the same name; it was the same man. I was thoroughly shocked.

Not only had my old therapist been invested in some kind of sick manipulation of me, but also he had managed to have several of these sexual relationships with his other clients. Now, on top of everything else, I felt betrayed. Back then, I had really thought he loved me. When I realized he had been using me, at least I comforted myself with the idea that somehow I was "special." Now I was not even the only one.

This group facilitator/ doctor asked me if I would be willing to give testimony for a disbarring hearing, along with the two other women. He explained that with three of us together, we had the power to have Dr. Trayer's license revoked, something that none of us could do very effectively alone. I wanted very much to join with them and take some action, but I was scared.

Talking about it in the group later that night, I decided to say no. I had recently heard awful stories of women whose credibility was brought into question, about how their whole sexual history was brought to trial when they pressed charges. I knew simply that I could not withstand this kind of "blame the victim" investigation, interrogation and humiliation. I just wasn't strong enough to put myself through it.

Now, I read over hospital notes from that time. There is a sense of coming full circle with it. Sharon, who is my investigating officer, says that what he did was wrong. No matter my desire and decision to go along with his suggestions, "No matter if I had been dancing naked on his desk" she said, "he was in the wrong because it was his place to keep the relationship strictly therapeutic and professional." I was the client. He was the psychiatrist. He had clearly abused his power, she told me. Still, it is reassuring to hear the voice of somebody else's reason. Still, the shame wants to push heavily in on my chest.

The two attorneys from the licensing board found him practicing in a nearby town, which I understand now is common practice for physicians with problems in their records. They interviewed, confronted him and he denied ever knowing me, ever having a client with my name (they used my married and maiden names, both). He said he had never been sexual with any of his clients. The attorney who made phone calls to my own three witnesses said their recall had been weak and sketchy. I could not describe the distinguishing marks he had on his body, though I remember my moment of discovery. In the end, my case was decided "not strong enough" to investigate further.

I was very disappointed, angry. The system seems so stacked to protect the professionals and placate the clients. I did gain though, in that I reclaimed much of my sacrificed power. But for me, it is not over yet. My mother had an old expression that fits perfectly here. She used to say, "The wheels of justice turn exceedingly slow, but they grind exceedingly fine." The wheels are turning and grinding. I am biding my time and open to discovering the way. It is close at hand. Perhaps telling this part of my story, refusing to protect him any longer, is the beginning of it.

During this period shortly after my divorce, I began to ask myself in earnest, "Who am I?" and "What is the way?" There were so many aspects to my life that I was trying to understand. Being a single mother with children ages 3, 4 & 6 kept me physically exhausted and emotionally drained.

I was a welfare recipient, living on $375.00 a month from the "Aide to Dependent Children" fund. The father of my children made two child support payments in seven years. Being dependent on welfare was totally degrading and frustrating, as it was a constant crisis of asserting myself within a system structured to strip away my rights and my power. I was in the process of leaving my church and had not yet been able to fill that void with anything spiritually nourishing. I did begin reading about world religions and was just starting to lean toward the field of metaphysics.

At this point in my life, I was also drinking a lot of wine and smoking a lot of dope. I became interested again in writing poetry and in keeping a journal. I was awakening to music. With a small inheritance from my grandfather, I bought a piano. It was clunky and very used. I "antiqued" it yellow/brown and stored it in my enclosed, but cold, back porch. When the children were napping, I'd play (my gloves on), my eyes closed, letting out all of the agony and beauty from deep inside me.

Having ended the sexual/romantic relationship with my therapist, I buried myself now, in secret shame. It left me with no one—no therapist, no lover, no adult to be close to. My loneliness was excruciatingly painful. My children were a godsend to me at this time, in spite of the work of taking care of them. One of their delightful discoveries in nature or about their own ability sent waves of pleasure through me, too. The spontaneous and easy affection we shared helped my heart be well. Their deep connection to me, and with each other, called me to participate in a circle of family that was lively and full. I was being needed, wanted.

I was even being appreciated. One night with my children, as they got into their pajamas, I was alone with my youngest, then about four, while he brushed his teeth and went to the toilette. There was a warmth between us that was just precious. He looked up at me and said, so sweetly, "Mom, I'm glad your here". I knew he was thanking me for being alive, for being at home with him right at that moment and not in the hospital.

Of course, the love of three children wasn't enough and I had very little else to keep me going. There were to be two more trips to the hospital to have my stomach pumped and three or four more admissions to psychiatric wards. I had access now, only to the free County Hospital Emergency Room and the Milwaukee County Mental Health Center, (then) North Division. These were the most difficult times of being hospitalized. By now I was becoming thoroughly "institutionalized" though I had never heard of the word or the concept. Going back into the hospital, when things "out here" in my life were too hard, too confusing, too painful, too difficult to cope with, became my way to signal "defeat."

While I did feel some immediate relief from the pressures in my life by "going back in," it really did not "help" me. It was not what would be referred to now, as "therapeutic," it was effective only in it's basic ability to keep me from killing myself. In fact, those days and nights on psychiatric wards have hurt me, in many small but significant ways that only now I'm beginning to identify and to understand. Yet at that time (1970) it was all there was, all I knew to turn to. I was 28 years old, desperate and alone.

Now, almost twenty-five years later, as I prepared to present my testimony against Dr. Trayer to the Wisconsin State Medical Licensing Board, I sent for copies of records from my many hospitalizations. In fact, they don't say a lot about me (the individual therapy notes through the years are much more interesting). But certain phrases, names, dates and medications I was on trigger the uncoiling of so many long forgotten, intensely painful memories, that I am almost "back there again." With a heightened sensitivity, I experienced my next few hospitalizations within a broader frame of reference.

At this point in my process, I was beginning to know that I was just one more person, like many I saw around me, who was trying to get something I needed from a system that operated in a distancing, blaming, punishing way and that all of our chances for success were very slim. At the beginning of this "mental illness" thing, I had hoped that there would be "help" and I would get well. By this point I was close to realizing that neither the help or the wellness would come to pass while "on the inside" and I did not know any other way. I felt confused, angry and afraid.

* * *

The first of these admissions to MCMHH, was right after leaving Dr. Trayer's office with my sister Sally. I had been in the bathroom, frantically trying to cut myself with a sewing scissors, while she filled him in on my behavior over the last few days. Back in his office, he gave me an injection to "calm me down." Again, he explained that if I "signed myself in" he wouldn't be able to treat me but he did say that he would come to visit. I knew I needed to be "in-patient" again and I voluntarily admitted myself.

This was my introduction to "Milwaukee County Mental Health Hospital"; long hall ways, gray concrete floors, dark woodwork, many doors, wide window sills, tall windows with thick mesh safety screens on the inside. The television set was behind a mesh screen like a cage with a door on it, up high on a shelf in the "day room." That's where the ping pong table was and all day long, the hollow sound of "pop, pop, pop" filled every corner of the room. I'd feel mad that some of the patients could be so unaffected by the annoying sound, they'd actually be having fun.

Some of the older women were intent on their knitting, oblivious to everything else around them. I wished I had something to do to distract me from being here. We sat on bright orange, molded plastic chairs, lined up on outside walls of the room. It felt like a gym, with florescent lights, everything so stark and hard there was an echo. At the end of the hall was a big, black, heavy gate that got pushed together, like an accordion, whenever someone was allowed to come in or go out of the ward.

I had waited for a very long time, for the one friend I had in the world to come and see me. Slowly, I started to let myself know that he was not ever going to show up, that he was not ever going to help me. I got mad. I got very, very mad (as he had taught me to do). I yelled and started to throw things around and I ripped my clothes and I screamed how I hated him. I fought back when they tried to pin me down (two male orderlies and then one big, fat nurse). I scratched and I kicked and I yelled as I lay in the middle of the hall on the floor. It felt good to fight back!

Then they dragged me across the floor to a little room with a high table, where they tied me down. The damn nurse was leaning over me, her face right in mine, being angry and insulting me with her yelling voice. She gave me a shot to "subdue me" (now known to me as a "chemical restraint"). What a horrible, helpless feeling that was, to be subjected to her abusive "power over" and then to feel myself going steadily down, down, down—totally against my own will.

I remember after that, being put on a chair in the long hallway, my arms crossed in front and wrapped around me in the white cloth bandages that I later learned was a "straight jacket". Here I was, blurry eyed and still, starring into space just like the other patients I had seen in the last several days. I too was silent. I had nothing to say. I didn't know why I was being punished, but I knew that I was and I didn't want to go through the whole ordeal again. Now, I was scared.

I became "the good patient", the compliant patient. I hated it there. I didn't know if I'd ever get out/ be allowed to go home. I held everything inside: my sadness, my anger, my fears. I tried to obey the rules, though I wasn't sure quite what they were. I remember agreeing to be "good," and the restraints were taken off of me. I ate what I was told to eat (everything tasted like cardboard). I took their pills when they were given, in little white paper cups, and I drank their horrible, watered down lemonade.

I went to bed when they told me to, but often I couldn't fall asleep. Sometimes I'd get back up and ask if I could sit in the day room. It was quiet in there then and it felt so very good to finally be alone. But after 15 minuets or so, they gave me more pills and I'd have to go back and get in my bed. I just longed for the dark. The dorm room didn't have a door and the bare light bulb in the hall shined right into my eyes. I'd try to find some little dark place when I'd turn on my side, put my face up close to the wall.

Too soon it would be daylight again. I got up when I was told to. Mornings were the worst part of my day. Nothing held any meaning for me anymore. I just did as I was told, like a mute zombie, because I was afraid not to. I had seen what they could do. Looking back on it all, is a long, lonely, lost blur in my mind. One time of being there slips into another. I was always cold. I remember asking for sweaters. Here, too, we were issued housedresses and underwear, but we were allowed to keep and wear our own shoes.

The bathroom stalls didn't have doors on them. That always made me uncomfortable. A matron would stand across the room, looking up and down the long row of stalls, making sure we weren't doing anything in there but going to the toilet. On one of my inpatient stays, I had recently gotten dentures. I remember how humiliating it was to have to take my teeth out while I brushed, hunching over a small sink as best as I could to give myself some degree of privacy.

When a doctor occasionally walked down the long hallway, everyone would try to talk to him. They'd hold out and wave their hands, calling "Doctor, Doctor, just one question please, just five minutes, please." or "Help me, help me," cried out from someone's old wounds within. The doctors, with their white lab coats over tailored blue or gray suits, would walk through the wards quickly, without making eye contact with any of us. It was as if to say, "I can not see you, I can not hear you" to no one in particular, but all of us felt the discount. Some of the patients got indignant or more insistent. I learned early on to not even try. My way was to simply sit quietly and wait for my turn.

Usually I had two 15 minute appointments with a doctor each week. I never knew whom they were going to be with, or remembered doctors from one time to the next. When I did talk with them I often felt confused, as if there were some hidden agenda they all had and my job was to guess at it. Being tested/evaluated, was always the worst. The questions were the same, but I struggled with the answers to them like each time was the first. I tried so hard, wanted so much to get it "right" so they would know that I was okay, that I didn't belong here, that I wasn't "crazy".

"Count backward by sevens from 100" or "Who were the last three presidents?" or "Tell me what it means to live in a glass house." I always felt so stupid! My math was terrible; I never did know what was going on in the outside world (or care, particularly) and the parables always seemed to be cryptic and complicated. It seemed to me that with each question I answered, I dug myself into the muck of "mental illness" deeper. "Now I'll never get out of here," played often through my mind after these kinds of failures.

There were many nights I sat in the big, cold, room with all the chairs, trying to imagine a place to escape to where I could find relief from the constantly blasting TV. The nurse would unlock the cage around the television set and pick the station we would watch. I'd watch the other patients and not know why I was here or what to do to get my self home again or even if that's what I wanted.

During the day I stood in long lines outside the nurses station. At 10:00 am, 12:00 noon, 2:00 PM and 4:00 PM, they would open the top half of the double door (it made a counter to lean on) and hand each of us one of our cigarettes, light it and tell us to "Move over for the next one." In the day room, I'd watch other women embroider dresser scarves. I found out one time, that I could get a "pass" for a 15 minute walk outside on the grounds, with a volunteer in a pink jacket. The quiet was wonderful.

Once, as I walked down the hall, I saw nurses in white uniforms playing cards with the patients and laughing, joking with each other. I wanted to "fit in" with them or to get their attention for me, but I didn't know how. The next thing I remember, I was being put into a long, deep tub of warm water. The tan canvass cover closed with a heavy zipper and just my head stuck out of a hole made in the fabric. I turned to my right and saw another woman in a tub next to me, just the same. We were in a green tiled shower room. The nurse who was turning on and off the hot water into the tub said it was called "hydrotherapy" and it was to calm us. It all seemed very unreal.

There were so many times like that, that felt "strange" when I was being hospitalized. It was as if floating through someone else's dream or caught in one of those "Snake Pit" kind of movies. Thinking back, I realize it was probably the drugged state I was in, as in the not so long ago early seventies, psychiatric patients were still being heavily medicated. It was an extremely traumatic experience each time I was in. This loss of my "other life" became overwhelming and I totally lacked confidence in my ability to sort it all out. Of course, just hanging on from one crisis to the next, I had absolutely no resiliency with which to cope. I was scared too, scared of just about everything that happened "in there."

Two or three of my hospitalizations were in an old, old building that is no longer used for patient services. (I passed it yesterday, driving slowly and really looking at it, sitting up on the hill in the sunshine). Often when I am out on what used to be called "The County Hospital Grounds" and now, some thirty years later is "Milwaukee Medical College and Froetdert Hospital/Clinic Campus," I try to catch a glimpse of it. Like an emotional tie or umbilical cord, old memories pull me toward the physical structure itself. The long tiled hallways, the folding metal gate, the long windows that opened only to the gray glare, come easily floating back into my mind.

I was working with a therapist about seven years ago at an outpatient clinic ran by the hospital. It was a very painful and cathartic experience to revisit those years of being treated in some of the same offices on the East Side and of being "locked up" by the same institution. The therapist remembered the name of the building; the old "North Division." Oh, it felt good to have someone else know what the place was like. Yesterday, I was surprised to see that it was just a big, old building, up on a hill, where the grass was a beautiful green. Not gone, but much less imposing, is the old, gray ghost.

Then there was the "new building," across a busy street. One day we were corralled into a little white bus. It was old and creaky and only big enough for six or eight of us. I didn't know where we were being taken and it never occurred to any of us that we had the right to ask. After a short drive we were unloaded. We'd reached our destination, the new building across the street that everybody had been talking about for weeks. In addition to psychiatric units, it also housed a big gym. Led past the modern circular bench and to the bright orange elevators, we were taken to play volleyball for an hour and a half. The opposing team was women from some other ward, equally drugged and uninterested in hitting a ball or moving quickly. Of course, we were not given the option to say no. Not having choices was one of the minor agonies of my hospitalization.

I revisited this place, too. Several days before my drive past North Division, my niece and I shared the responsibility of admitting my sister Sally to a psychiatric ward. The "Crisis Center" was around the back of the building. It wasn't until I joined her children for a family session and we walked in through the front door that I realized I was again walking down red brick hallways, past the wooden circular bench and standing in front of the bright orange elevators. I grabbed my nephew's near, strong arm and whispered, "Oh my god, I've been here before." He gently reassured me that they couldn't make me stay that I, too, would be leaving with him in about an hour. Having left here for the last time at that point, more than twenty some years before, I was shocked to still be so intimidated by the power of the place and the extent of the flashback to my own fear and helplessness.

Having to bring my sister in was hard enough, but bearable that first night because this is what she wanted. But now, seeing her so afraid, powerless, frail, confused, physically and mentally distraught, dependent on the mercy of "the system," broke my heart. Enough that I had been there. Too much, that now she was in the same place. One of our older brothers, Bob, had been here too way before me. The three of us understood each others' sense of "being the troubled one, the one who was not quite right, the one who was different than, the one who couldn't quite cope, the one to be afraid of or for, the one who was the black sheep." Being "the one who…" each of us felt a special compassion for and comfort in each other. Had it been an option for them, in the 1920's, 30's and 40's, would our parents have been here too?

I do not think that anyone can truly know the awful powerlessness of being locked up in a mental institution unless they have been there. It was bad enough for me to have absolutely no self esteem, no sense of inner worth, no belief in my ability to affect change, both in and around me and no hope in any kind of saving grace coming in from outside of me. But then, to be locked behind metal gates and bolted doors, as if in punishment for my lack, totally and completely stripped me of any sense of personal power and the dignity of personal freedom.

Of course, in this setting, the more subtle forms of coercion and control almost go unnoticed because they are so commonplace; the straight jackets, the ankle cuffs, the isolation rooms, the tie down rings on the sides of a table, the injections and medications by mouth, to subdue. These were the daily, sometimes hourly rituals of "treatment" for the many of us who have been mentally ill and warehoused, now in what we can safely call "the past." It was an ugly and often abused system of "power over" used to manipulate, to re-train and to punish us. That anyone at all survives it, is a miracle; yet not without it's life long lessons seared into our souls. We are never again the same.

* * *

It had been a year and a half since my first stay at North Division, where I waited to be rescued by my "lover/priest/god/the father/psychiatrist." I had finally confided my terrible truth to a new psychiatrist, the first woman in a therapeutic role that I had seen. I remember that last staffing, when I was being released into my mother's care and she sat by my side as friend and confidant. The conditions of my leaving were laid out, i.e.: "That I put an immediate end to my relationship with Dr. Trayer and that I find and begin outpatient treatment with a new and reputable psychiatrist."

Mom and I left later that morning and she drove me away from the hospital in her little yellow Pinto. As I sat silently and looked over the huge expanse of County Hospital grounds and then fed into Hwy.#100, I began to have a sense of where I had been, geographically. The transition back into the mainstream (other cars whizzing by office buildings, restaurants, stop lights, etc.) was both exhilarating and frightening for me. I was moving so fast, into this other reality. I wasn't sure I was ready, could find or make my way in this outer world.

Within months I was back in the hospital again. It was around my birthday time and nearing Christmas. I was lonely, discouraged and worn out. I was trying to be a good parent (single parenting hadn't yet caught on as a community support project) to my three children, ages 3, 4, and 6. I had been stigmatized now as a "welfare mom" in our small village of middle and working class people. I was being matronized by my own three sisters, for being poor (they resented mom helping me financially), divorced (the first in my Catholic family), and mentally ill (they saw it as a "cop out" from responsibility and of course had nothing to do with my older brother's mental illness or our common family system that might just have been a bit dysfunctional). It was hard to "hold my head up."

I had tried therapy again but had given up (thinking I was being mis-diagnosed and mis-understood by the therapist who tried to draw out my anger, my sense of outrage about the sexual abuse). No psychotherapy also meant not any stabilizing medication. In desperation, late one night, I took a couple of handfuls of aspirin. I think that I was taken by ambulance (like admissions, "ambulance rides I had" slip into one another and it's hard to have separate and distinct memories) to the County Hospital emergency room. I had my stomach pumped, now a frequent necessity (flash backs, the taste of charcoal and those damn tubes being threaded up my nose and down the back of my throat, gagging, panicking while they just said, "Keep swallowing"). Later I was admitted to North Division for "emergency detention."

Staffing notes from that time say, "There have been four other prior suicidal gestures. At the time of admission, patient states that she terminated with Dr. Trayer one month ago. She describes herself as being an insecure, lonely, dependent individual who since her divorce from her husband has had many involvements with boyfriends who appear to reject her, resulting in her depression and states of loneliness. She describes her involvement with Dr. Trayer as not being productive, as in order to "attend to him, she put aside her own psychological needs."

On my last trip "in" I was hospitalized against my will. I had begun an impetuous (reactionary) relationship after ending the affair with my psychiatrist. Enroute to another city for his next job, this man lived with me for a few weeks and he and I became engaged, complete with family announcements, a party to celebrate and all. Love letters followed, then for weeks, nothing. When I finally tracked him down by phone, he told me he was sorry but that he discovered he didn't want to marry me. I was devastated! I couldn't stop crying. After several days like this, I called my mom and asked her to stay with me for awhile, take care of my children. All I wanted was to have everyone leave me alone, just let me cry.

Mom felt scared with the level of my emotional pain and my non-stop crying. After being with me a day or so, she called my sister who lived near-by. Sally and her husband suddenly arrived that night and the two of them took me by the arms and forced me into their car, me being angry and resisting all the way. They drove me back to the hospital I had left just four months earlier. I clearly remember the terrible indignity that I felt. When refusing to "sign myself in," I was told by the examining psychiatrist that he had the power to sign the admission papers that gave MCMHC permission to hold me for a three day observation period (for my own good, of course, in light of my history of suicide attempts) and after that I could continue to be held there by a court order.

I realized that in spite of what I knew about myself (that I was not going to kill myself, I just felt terribly sad and angry and wanted to do my grieving) and in spite of what I knew about what I needed (freedom from child care responsibilities and a safe, nurturing environment in which to rest and heal), my wants and needs, my intuition and my will, were not going to be considered. I was no longer "in-charge of my life" however haltingly I put that into practice. I realized that at the most basic level of being able to say "no," I had no power. This was hitting bottom for me. I felt myself just simply giving up.

I acquiesced to the giving over of my watch, ring, and chain, dropping them into the torn brown envelope held out to me by the matron. I stood in the tepid pre-admission shower, washing with a strong, smelly disinfectant liquid soap. I underwent the humiliating strip search, body cavities suspect as hiding places for weapons or drugs, told to squat, to bend over in front of her. I obediently gave the accounting of my bruises and history of disease. I felt numb, detached, not really there.

It was a holding/observation ward. I was now in the new building. There were a few men sitting around in front of the TV. They taught me how to roll my own cigarettes, showed me the little red leather rolling machine next to the blue can of tobacco with a picture on it. It was a weekend. Everything was moving very slowly. I wouldn't be assigned a psychiatrist until Monday, then probably admitted to a regular in-patient ward. I waited it out. I tried to be "good" i.e.; compliant.

I remember walking back and forth in that long L-shaped hallway. The more I walked, the more restless I got. Edging now towards the opposite end of the emotional walkway I felt trapped in; I started to feel really angry, really furious. How dare they lock me up, hold me here, "observe me", make me wait until Monday to tell my story, get some help, get out of here! I knew I couldn't wait anymore. I needed something to happen now, right now!

Standing by myself, down at the long end of the hallway, away from the nurses' station, it seemed perfectly logical that I bang my head against the concrete block wall. My head bounced back. It made a hollow sound, louder than I thought it would be. I banged my head against the wall again. I did it again and again, as hard as I could. I don't remember falling to the floor. It seemed like instantly there were nurses and orderlies bending over me.

When I "came to" I was in a small room with a door that was right across from me. The door had a small window in it and that, too, had it's own little door. My bed was up high, almost like an operating table in the middle of the room. I couldn't move my arms and then I noticed that I couldn't move my legs either. In a little while an intern stood up, who had been sitting on a chair next to me. He explained, very gently, what had happened. I had knocked myself out in the hallway and now I was in an isolation room and tied down so I couldn't hurt myself anymore. He said he had been waiting there, for me to "wake up."

I don't know how long I was in isolation or in restraints. It seemed like a long time to me. My tongue was thick, my head hurt, I had been heavily medicated. I was left alone now. Every once-in-a-while someone would open the little window and look in. I remember hearing the loud click, click rhythm of the window door opening and closing. I felt angry that I was here, that I didn't know who or why someone was looking at me, that I couldn't do anything about it. None of it made any sense to me; here I was, lying on my back, strapped down to a high, hard table in the middle of an empty room.

The intern, or perhaps another one, now came in to feed me my meal with a spoon. I hated it. Not having even one hand free to feed myself or even push the spoon away. I felt like a prisoner, not a patient; someone who had done something terribly wrong and was now being punished by being in "isolation", (which was where I had been all of my life, steeped in shame). This hospital was not a benevolent place, a place of healing. I wanted to get out of here and I couldn't imagine how. I had to ask for a bedpan and be helped on and off it, wiped. The intern gave me more pills, sips of water through a straw. I was alone again, lying there, not moving. Sleep was my only escape.

Next thing I remember, it was Monday morning and I knew this was my only chance. I found myself sitting in a small office, pleading my case with an Asian doctor I had never seen before. I wasn't even sure if he would understand my language. I told him that I did not want to stay, did not think that I needed to be there, had experienced all of my power being stripped away and now I wanted it back. Yes, I was very sad and very angry. No, I did not want to take it out on myself. No, I did not feel suicidal. I said that I wanted to go home, to take care of my children, to continue to grieve, to think about finding a therapist, to help myself heal, to get well on my own. I was discharged that afternoon. I had said all the right things. It was a victory.

That was my last trip into the hospital. Being forced to leave my home, get into a car, be taken to a psychiatric admissions unit, being held there against my will, frightened and confused—being made totally dependent on others, punished for what little will I did exert and having to wait out my time there, so terribly alone, no advocate by my side—fighting for my freedom with one more psychiatrist who did not know me, yet had the power to unlock the door or keep me hostage in his institution—being there in that way at that time of my development, was a significant turning point for me.

I decided that I would never again allow myself to give up control over my mental, emotional and physical state of being and that I would never again allow anyone else in my life to have so much power over me that they could take away my freedom.

That was the end of my 5 1/2 years of bouncing in and out of psychiatric hospitals. It was the end of using heavy medication. It was also the end of my doing psychotherapy for awhile. It was the very beginning of my determination and my ability to focus my own strengths in the service of my healing. I had come home. I made peace with my mother. I tried to reassure my children that, this time, I was staying home. We had to work out angers. There were lots of tears and hugs in the weeks to come. Yet, there was hope. We had another chance together and I wanted to make it right for their sake as well as my own.

Chapter Two

Postpartum Depression

I don't know exactly when I first heard the term "postpartum depression" but I know it was during one of my longer courses of therapy. I was filling in details of my mental health history and talking about having a "nervous breakdown" several months after the birth of my last child. The therapist commented, "Oh, postpartum depression." In hearing a little about what it was, I realized that what I had gone through had a name, a predictable course, a set of recognizable symptoms and that other women had experienced it too. Hearing the medical term was like finding chunks of glittering gold lying on the bottom of a pan full of silt and sand. I needed only to sift through medical journals and books about pregnancy and giving birth, to find out more, to understand. What a comfort it was to hear that this happened to other mothers like me. Maybe it wasn't some failing on my part after all.

That was in the early 70's and was about what I had been through six or seven years before. I didn't learn or even hear much more about the illness after that, yet I noticed health care professionals nod their head when I rolled the words easily off my tongue. I liked appearing to understand from a medical point of view. It offered me some sense of power now, in what had been a totally powerless situation. I never talked about the guilt and shame that went with it. I had felt like such a "bad mother" by not being able to do my job, by having to leave my children during my hospitalizations. I felt especially heart broken in not being able to take care of my new baby myself. This small, precious infant who needed me, who had a right to have me with him with those familiar smells, tone of my voice, the body that had held him and held him still through those long and hard nights of crying, his and mine.

During those years I felt so torn. I had wanted more than anything to provide the nurturing, the consistency, the feeling of safety to my children that I'd never had. Yet I was not able to. I felt such sad irony in being the cause of pain to them. I had wanted to right all the wrongs of my own childhood (though I was totally unaware of this emptiness that was driving me to be "the perfect mother") and I believed that if I only tried hard enough, I could. Instead, I have repeated some of the same old parental patterns and made new mistakes as well. Now 35 years later, I continue to come to terms with the imperfections of my humanness, as well as the ramifications of my mental illness and how that has affected the shaping of my children's lives around my own.

By the time I gave birth to my third child, in 1966, I had been pregnant each year for four years in a row. Following the birth of my first baby, I miscarried with my second at five and a half months. I had fallen on an outing in the country on a Sunday afternoon and began hemorrhaging that night. My mother-in-law came to help and wrapped me in towels as I lay in the back seat of her car. Finally, in the emergency room when the attending physician stepped out, I insisted on seeing my baby, now in a silver basin with a white cloth over the top of it. My husband and I were able to say goodbye to this tiny, perfectly formed baby boy who was not meant to be. My heart was broken and I don't think I even knew it at the time. Those were the days when nobody talked about loss and grieving, especially in regard to childbirth and the expectation of new life. I just went home afterward, hugged my toddler and quietly cried. Our second daughter was born the following year and then our son.

Three months after giving birth for the last time, I had my "nervous breakdown" or what I now know as postpartum depression (P.P.D.) Unlike the more commonly known "baby blues" that leave one crying often and feeling totally worn out—my symptoms didn't go away after a week or two. I was one of about 15% of new mothers in which the "blues" deepen into a more serious and lasting depression. I cried all of the time and was exhausted but unable to sleep for most of the first weeks. I felt guilty in what I thought was my own inadequacy in giving my baby what he needed (for surely if he were getting what he needed from me, he wouldn't be crying so constantly).

My older two were suffering the results as well of what I thought was my ineffective mothering. I had no more energy to give. Trying to fill the day long basic needs of my children plus making meals, doing dishes, washing diapers, making formula, picking up the clutter in the house and giving baths at night was all that I could manage in a usual 16-18 hour day. I was physically and mentally exhausted. I pulled into myself as much as I was able to, almost like trying to hide from these overwhelming outside demands. I was probably over-responsive to my children's emotional needs because I so very much wanted to be everything for all of them. I began to simply do what I had to do with a kind of rote determination. Nothing was enjoyable anymore.

I was feeling terribly lonely in my life and very much alone in my marriage. My husband did not know how to give me support; in fact, I don't think the thought of doing that ever occurred to him. He himself was overwhelmed. He handled that by finding excuses to be away from home and from the stress of his responsibilities more and more as the weeks went on. My isolation grew worse because I did not have even one friend, one other woman to fall back on, to tell my troubles to or share my feelings with. When finaly I did "fall apart" I turned to my sister and my mom for the understanding and the "hands on" help that I needed. I had been trying to do it all, all alone and to do it perfectly. I had waited way too long to ask for help.

* * *

Now, more than thirty-five years later, as I look back to explore my postpartum depression, I begin to put the pieces together of what then was only a complicated and confusing puzzle. A picture begins to emerge for me of who I was then and of what was happening in my body/mind.

I am learning that the hormone estrogen, which heightens sensitivity to neurotransmitters that influence mood, rises 25-30% during pregnancy and drops to normal immediately after birth. The brain has receptors for estrogen and for another ovarian hormone, progesterone. In the days before menstruation, hormone secretion also changes rapidly and there is some evidence that women like me, who have experienced what is now called "premenstrual syndrome", have a higher than average rate of postpartum disorders.

For over four consecutive years, my rapid hormone changes during pregnancy and especially at the time of childbirth, had been a source of extreme mood fluctuation. "For some women, moods may be especially susceptible to hormonal effects immediately after delivery and the resulting instability can deepen into a persistent depression for other reasons as well."

"Postpartum disorders" (the baby blues, postpartum depression and postpartum psychosis) are sometimes considered a product of our modern industrial society which supposedly makes childbirth a medical condition, deprives women of support from extended families, allows no time for mothers' rest and seclusion and had abandoned traditional rituals of transition."

"A woman susceptible to feelings of inadequacy will find it especially difficult to care for a demanding and difficult child and she often will feel like she is failing as a mother and become depressed." Both of my last two babies were temperamental, easily upset, had trouble sleeping for long periods and cried a lot. Studies have shown that "Children evaluated just after birth (to exclude the possibility that the infants behavior resulted from the mothers' depression) who were irritable, with restless and irregular body movements, had mothers who were more likely to be depressed two months later—whatever her own mood just after delivery." said the Harvard Mental Health Letter.

A study at Emery University in Atlanta found that both depressed mothers and their babies have increased amounts of the hormone cortisol in their blood, an indication of stress. Such high levels can make these infants vulnerable to over-reacting to stress later in life. And health experts say that women with a personal or family history of depression are more likely to experience postpartum depression. Women are also at greater risk if they have experienced postpartum depression in an earlier pregnancy.

Other stresses at the time included the fact that my husband and I had very little money and I struggled daily, wondering how to pay for groceries and warding off bill collectors. One of my hospital intake records reminds me that during my first crisis, I had disconnected the doorbell and the telephone ringer. It was too hard to pretend I wasn't there to them when the children heard the ringing and asked me why I wasn't answering the door or phone.

Meanwhile, my husband was gambling like he used to do aboard ship in the Navy when he would come home with only a small part of a paycheck. Now it was at the pool hall or the bowling alley or on the golf course. He often asked me to "call in sick" for him and then he'd pack up his golf clubs or bowling bag and be gone. It was hard enough for me to be raising three children virtually alone, but worse because of the constant hurt I felt in having a husband who was much more concerned with his own wants and needs than he was with the rest of the family's.

I guess I had hoped that the arrival of each of our last two children would change our unhappy marriage and when that didn't, I was disappointed over and over. Eventually, having to give up what little hope I had led directly to my "hitting bottom" again. The intake records say that I had been in the basement that time, washing diapers. Someone found me, crouched down on the floor in a corner. There had been wood frame and chicken wire storage compartments in the apartment building. I choose the corner of ours to hide in. I remember wishing I would never have to go upstairs again.

In my research, I am finding out that postpartum depression is fairly comon, though not well understood and often is misdiagnosed. Left untreated, the depression can become postpartum psychosis and can lead to suicide and infanticide. Newspaper headlines and television specials are filled with such stories: "Mother drowns two children in a car." "Mother drowns five children in the bathtub." "Mother kills self on railroad tracks." "Mother stabs fetus in toilet." "Mother drowns baby and throws body in lake." Some mothers in profound depression, at the end of their pregnancy, feel extremely inadequate and want to kill themselves. One mother who was estatic when she found out she was pregnant, later fell to her death from a twelfth floor. She said, "I am useless and rotten. My heart is broken. Please forgive me." Another mother has been sentenced to be in prison until she is eighty years old. She says, "I have been sentenced to a doomed life." Another mother could face the death penalty, because of her very serious postpartum depression. Mothers who kill their children are seldom released to psychiatric hospitals. Postpartum psychosis is just now being considered an insanity legal defense. Their mothers kill 200 children each year.

Perhaps we can understand slightly better now, what might causes a mother to turn against her children. The popular myth is that when you have a baby you should be at your best and blossoming. But for 15% of all women who give birth, the months after delivery offer a profound sense of sadness, hopelessness, mood swings and insomnia. "For a variety of reasons, childbirth can trigger severe depression in some women, making it difficult for them to take care of themselves and the infant that needs round the clock attention," says Sylvia Wood in her article in the *Albany Times Union*. Deborah Fischel, interviewed on a recent

Oprah Winfry show about the topic, says that the illness follows a continuem. In postpartum depression what the mother experiences is real and if moving into a postpartum psychosis, her altered perception feels real to her but it is not.

Because of the profound sense of shame a new mother feels, she seldom is able to let others around her know that she needs help. The social work manager at Bellevue Women's Hospital near Albany, says, "Often the woman feels ashamed, thinking, "the baby is fine, why do I feel this way?" "The women themselves know that something is very wrong. It seems to be the nature of the disease that one can't say anything about it to others. Yet the depression and the violent thoughts are not normal and if left untreated, they will not go away. The new mother is overtired and stressed, her brain is pushed to an abnormal state and along with the hormonal shifts, the mother sees herself becoming very different than how she used to be. There often is a disconnect between the mother and the child. The woman seldom tells her husband what is going on. Often the intervention comes only after some tragedy and the new mother is seen in the emergency room of a hospital.

These women need treatment. Postpartum depression can occur anytime within the first year of the baby's birth. Undiagnosed mental health problems can surface during this time and causes are usually one's own history or one's family history. The illness cycles into "crazy" ways of thinking. Perceptions of the world outside the self are frightening and can set off violent behavior. The woman experiencing P.P.D. most often needs to be protected from herself. New medications, in some cases electric shock therapy and psychotherapy can begin the long-term course of treatment for postpartum depression and postpartum psychosis. There is hope. A major part of the problem with postpartum illness has been in diagnosing it. Yet once diagnosed, it is almost always treatable. In the last ten or fifteen years, as we have begun to talk about this, treatment is more available.

Several years ago Marie Osmond appeared on Oprah Winfry's television program and has written about her journey out of postpartum depression. She talked about her despair and her emotional frailty that had taken over her daily existence. She says, "If I could just be honest about what it was like for me, then perhaps it would help another woman describe it to her doctor or husband or children." Then later, during her second appearance on the show, she said that the response to her initial appearance on *Oprah* told her there were thousands of other women who had experienced much the same thing. Marie said that it is time for us to start taking care of ourselves body, mind, heart and soul and to learn to develop boundaries so that we can protect ourselves. She suggested that as individuals, when we begin to count ourselves as important, then together we have a strong chance of finding some solutions to this. I very much appreciate her courage to risk telling her story.

Treatment, for me, had to be emergency hospitalization. I had simply reached the point where I was no longer able to function. Hiding under my sister's kitchen table, huddled there with my children by my side, I was declaring my inability to cope with anything more. The promise of being able to hide legitimately within the safety of a psychiatric "womb" where I would be taken care of: nurtured, fed and allowed to rest, sounded like a warm "Mother kind of Heaven" to me. Finally, I could let down and be the "child" (the starving/ neglected/ lonely child) that I always was inside.

Later came the interviewing, the testing, and the diagnosis. At first, it was "manic-depressive schizophrenia," which many years later, I understood was the "catch all" diagnosis of the times. Today I would have been diagnosed with clinical major depression. Psychiatric drugs were prescribed for me, as well as vitamins and medication to help me sleep. I worked with Dr. Trayer in his office at the Hill several times a week, to uncover what it was that might be causing me so much inner pain. In later months, E.C.T. (electro convulsive therapy) was recommended and in my case, I believe was responsible for pulling me back from my catatonic state. In subsequent hospitalizations, there was very little to no psychotherapy available and I was heavily medicated. I remember having difficulty in just plain walking, my feet weighted in psychotropic cement.

Slow as it seems, there has been progress in the last thirty-five years or so. E.C.T. is still being used, though with much more discrimination and is highly effective for severe depression or mania. Reports say that it can be safely administered a week after delivery.

High doses of oral estrogen, started immediately after delivery are sometimes used as a treatment for women with a history of severe postpartum depression. For new mothers who do not have to be hospitalized, "antidepressants may be taken even while breast feeding as the known risks to side effects in the child are rare." Recent research shows that both antidepressants and mood stabilizers can also prevent the development of postpartum disorders.

Of course, on-going one-to one psychotherapy, couple counseling, specifically geared support groups, coaching, pastoral consultations, spiritual enrichment gatherings and self help meetings (as in the 12 Step Programs) all are quite accessible in one's community these days even for low-income people. Group situations in particular are rich with resources and can provide new mothers or family members with the opportunity to relate to and learn from others who have had similar experiences. Two organizations that arrange support groups and educate about infant care and postpartum adjustment after delivery are: Depression After Delivery and Postpartum Support International.

We are learning some things as health care/human services professionals that can help prevent postpartum disorders (again, "baby blues, depression, manic depression and psychosis). They are; good prenatal care, reduction of stress during pregnancy, screening for a history of psychiatric disorders, attention to medical conditions that could cause psychiatric symptoms, reassurance to new mothers that "baby blues" are both common and temporary, educating family doctors or OB/GYN practitioners to ask about depressive symptoms and encouragement to families to seek out mental health professionals.

I know that if the clergy person I dragged my husband to for counseling could have come up with something more than his "blame the victim" advice to me, to "develop a more positive attitude" and to us, to "pray more," we might have been able to work this through much earlier in our marriage. Had he seen our family as a whole he might have suggested; that we have time together away from the children/ that both of us begin to work with mental health practitioners/ that we learn to build changes into our relationships with each other, our children, friends, family and that we strengthen our spiritual connections with a Power Greater in our lives. There could have been healing then and perhaps prevention of this traumatic impact on all of us as a family.

But then again, believing as I do in the higher plan and that nothing in this life is by "coincidence" or of "mistake"—I do know that we all (my ex-husband, our three children and myself) are exactly where we need to be and have traveled here exactly by the path that was opened before us.

* * *

It used to be hard to remind myself that my moods were felt easily by my children, without feeling shame and blame for how that was sure to have hurt them. In my process these days, of forgiving myself, I remember as well that my moods also brought them comfort and closeness and love. Because my children's father was most often absent, I became even more the emotional tone setter and they became the barometers that registered my state of heart and mind. Young ones are highly attuned to even slight nuances of a parent's changing emotional state because it is his or her wellbeing that the child is dependent on, for their own.

For my two daughters (one had just turned one, the other was almost three years old) it was an adjustment to have mommy suddenly go away and then bring back home another baby who obviously was going to stay. But then mommy started getting sick and "tired" all the time and they had even less of her, when they really needed the reassurance of more. They cried more easily, were pickier about what they ate, napped less peacefully and generally seemed "out of sorts" more often. My oldest seemed angry, as if she were trying to show me that she didn't need me anymore, that she could do things for and by herself. She especially wanted to take over the care of this new baby, which required a lot of tactful intervention by me. My youngest daughter simply wanted to cling, to be in my arms or on my lap or simply next to me, most of the time. My new baby took his bottle, slept well during the day and most often cried during the night.

My dwindling reservoir of physical strength, mental clarity and emotional resiliency was being depleted day by day. At night the oldest two would sleep soundly 'till morning, while I sat in the rocking chair holding the baby, both of us crying. I remember being in that little hallway between the bedrooms and the bathroom, trying absolutely everything I could think of to help my infant son and just praying that nobody else would wake up, which would mean more for me to deal with right then. During the day I was in touch by phone, with both my mother and sister for emotional support. Even I didn't realize how exhausted and out of control I was becoming, much less be able to give them a clue that I needed some help. It took my family and me by complete surprise, to find myself hiding under my sister's kitchen table that day and checking into a private psychiatric hospital that night.

Each child went to stay with their separate caretaker's full time, so their dad could continue to work during the day and be free in the evening. The baby was taken immediately to the home of friends of ours, through our church. The mom was a nurse and a mother herself and was best able to care for our little one at the time. When it began to look like I might be in treatment for some time, the decision was made for the children's paternal grandparents to make the trip here from Ohio and take the baby back home with them. I don't remember having any part in the decision making, and though it was probably the best choice, I felt very sad having my new baby so far away.

Longer-term plans were being made for the family to care for the older children too. My own mom took our one-year-old, who was still a baby herself, in. My mom's second husband (the only maternal grandfather the children have known) was gracious and affectionate. Stories came back to me of long hours he spent playing with our toddler and of her baby bed and favorite blankets and toys fitting right into their home. I've seen pictures of the diapers hanging to dry in Grandma's sunny back yard. I was glad my little one was there.

My older sister Sally, who lived nearby, took our three-year-old into her already full family of seven. There, the children ranging in age from two to twelve, welcomed her right in, trying to out-do each other as to who could "take the best care of" her. I know she felt the love there and had the opportunity of many advantages but I also know that she was confused and scared/angry. File notes from my psychiatrist (who interviewed me with my husband sometimes) report that when her dad came to visit, she would refuse to look at him or talk to him. It breaks my heart to read that now, when at the time I'd felt relieved because it seemed the perfect place for my sensitive first child.

The children were told simply that "mommy was sick," she would stay at the hospital for awhile and that when she was "all-better," everyone could come home and we would all be together again. My illness and the sudden changes that ensued must have been frightening for my three very young children. They had lost not only the primary caretaker in their lives, but because of that, everything else dear to them. They may have thought that I didn't want to be with them or even that it might have been their fault that I wasn't. I don't know.

I had very little contact with my children during the first year of my hospitalization. I'd be home for a day here and there, then weekends, or I'd be discharged and discover in a short time that I needed to be right back in again. We never had a chance as a family, to regain any sense of real stability. In addition, as my husband changed jobs over the years, we were frequently moving back and forth from his hometown to mine.

During my State Hospital stay in Ohio, the children were able to stay together with their Grandma and Grandpa there. Extended family members took them on outings and visited often, celebrated holidays with them, filled their basic needs and showered all three with love. Back here, during my several County Hospital admissions, the children were again able to stay together most of the time and to be at home while various family members came in to take care of them.

It was my hope that in those jarring and confusing times in the young and fragile lives of my children, they found comfort in the presence of so many family members who truly loved and took excellent care of them. In my absence at the time, I remember wishing that their innocent sense of involvement with "self" at the center, would help keep them resilient and "normalize" them. It has been of enormous healing to me to have noticed over the years, that my children have befriended, comforted, challenged and encouraged each other. There is a bond among them, born out of having to cope with the pain of so many losses and the difficulty of having to adjust to so much change. An opportunity was created for them to develop a very special, deep and abiding love with one another and they have. Perhaps this is the healing gift, born out of all the wounding. This bond has sustained, been a challenge to and re-generated hope in them, time after time. I am most pleased with what they together have made for themselves. I am graced, as well, with their ability to have also maintained and nurtured this bond with me and with their father.

Chapter Three

Family Of Origin

"Whether we, either counselors or clients, have succeeded in becoming a whole person depends a good deal on the families in which we grew up. Whether we can remain whole and continue to develop our potentials will depend on the families (or other intimate living networks) that we have created ourselves." says Sharon Wegscheider-Cruse in her early book on family therapy.

Wegscheider-Cruse goes on to talk about the family as a system and explains "Every system is [1] made up of component parts that are [2] linked together in a particular way [3] to accomplish a common purpose." These component parts are, of course, the family members and they work together to keep the system intact, which is the common purpose. Any threat to the particular way they work together is very stressful. After being disorganized by a threat, the whole family system slowly regains its stability.

She uses an analogy (that she says is borrowed in part from Virginia Satir) of a mobile. The mobile is a good image for actually seeing the system working. Imagine a stick with other sticks hanging from it. Then imagine eight paper triangles (my family of origin) hanging by string from several of the sticks. The shapes represent the family members and the sticks and string, the family rules. The mobile is designed to keep its balance. If it is caught by a wind (any kind of stress or change) it begins swinging and twisting. Then slowly, it brings itself back into order and balance.

That is the power and strength of the family. It can work for health and wholeness or to maintain or create the ill health and brokenness of its members. Intervention of any kind with any of the family members, including crisis counseling or assistance from a medical team, is extremely threatening to the existing order of the system. Everyone tries to quickly get back to the old and familiar pattern. Therefore, there is a built-in denial of problems, resistance to change and a need for everyone to remain within the parts they play out.

What links family members together are the rules. Wegscheider-Cruse says, "These rules determine the functions of each person, the relationships between persons, the goals toward which they all are heading, how they intend to get there and what will be required and forbidden along the way." The three basic rules in dysfunctional families are don't feel, don't trust and don't tell. We, who learn and become loyal to these rules, carry them out of the family system with us and into our continuing lives.

Along with the rules are the roles that family members maintain in order to keep the balance. These become individual dysfunctions that children learn and take with them when leaving the original family. These adults then attempt to carry out these roles for their lifetime because they know them so well. The roles are familiar, secure, and require little effort. Each one has emotional "payoffs" that seem to make them worthwhile. Wegscheider-Cruse says, "Family members eventually become addicted to their roles, seeing them as essential to survival." Inspite of the fact that these learned behaviors do not really help individuals get what they want with each other, they ward off the more threatening aspect of change. The "winds" disrupt what is known.

In her extensive work with alcoholic/dysfunctional families, Wegscheider-Cruse has given us names for these roles. These are the defenses that true feelings hide behind. These roles serve to protect the security of individuals in the family system they are dependent on. She says she has seen five basic roles played out and has named them: Enabler, Hero, Scapegoat, Lost Child and Mascot. All roles are played by someone and everyone plays a role, maybe several. Roles have to do with position in the family, rather than personality. This role-playing is happening subconsciously, outside of the awareness of the family members. The damage to individuals is in that they cannot be honest with themselves or others. They are forced to send double messages instead, one from the self in the role and another from the real person who is hurting inside.

In troubled homes, says Claudia Black, "Parents were not able to consistently attend to your needs and were not able to offer you a sense of emotional 'safety' and not able to help you believe you were special." She says these can be homes without an identifiable problem, homes where a family avoids feelings, where there is little nurturing, where rules are rigid and homes where time is not given to the children.

Black goes on to say, "Should alcoholism, physical or sexual abuse or mental illness have been part of your family, the consequences are even greater. Children of such families have difficulty asking for what they want, difficulty trusting and difficulty identifying or expressing feelings. It is common to have great fears of being rejected, resulting in a tremendous need to seek approval. An over-developed sense of responsibility is often characteristic. There are often fears of "losing control" while they demonstrate an extreme need to control." She adds, "Whether or not there was an identifiable problem in the family, the child has experienced loss in her childhood. That loss is very painful and for the loss to no longer have side effects in the adulthood, it needs to be addressed."

Wegscheider-Cruse quotes Virginia Satir's experience with families, "The atmosphere in a troubled family is easy to feel. Whenever I am with such a family, I quickly sense that I am uncomfortable. It is a sad experience for me to be with these families. I see the hopelessness, the helplessness, and the loneliness. I see the bravery of people trying to cover up—a bravery that can eventually kill them. There are those who are still clinging to a little hope, who can still bellow or nag or whine at each other. Others no longer care. These people go on, year after year, enduring misery themselves or in their desperation, inflicting it on others."

These unspoken yet very strict rules and roles were the guidelines in my family. I'm sure that they were also the guidelines in the families that my parents grew up in and their parents' families before them. I am coming to understand that most parents do the best they can with what they have to work with. My parents' ability was seriously limited by the trauma in their own young lives, most of which remained unexamined and unresolved. Knowing that helps tremendously in my being able to forgive them for damage that was done to me. I am in process with coming to acceptance of the long line of family dysfunction that has accumulated, damaging the lives of both of my parents, as well. It hurts deeply to imagine who each of them could have become, were it not for the burden of their own internal pain.

Had my family of origin been able to ask for and receive the help of family therapy, this is what we might have looked like in the therapists' office, at three separate stages of my life with them. It is an imaginary account, to be able to share with you a glimpse into the roles and rules we lived by over the years.

Almost Real Family Sculpture #1

Mom is sitting close to the male therapists' desk and crying. She has convinced all of us to be here today and she doesn't know where to begin telling our story. Mom is a beautiful woman who one time stood tall and carried herself proudly. Her bearing can be seen in how she still holds her shoulders and in the tilt of her chin. Today she is tired. She wears a simple maternity top, straight skirt and low pumps. She can say only, "I am so lonely."

Dad has on loose fitting gray trousers and wears argyles with his brown loafers. He too seems to have a carriage that says, "good breeding." He wears thin silver eyeglasses. His face is long and thin. His voice is low and he speaks slowly and deliberately. He clenches his jaw and sighs a lot, not knowing that he's noticed. I think he's angry but I'm not sure. He seems to prefer sitting a little off to the side of the rest of the family.

The Crazy Quilt

The five children are all in chairs pulled close to each other. Jane sits at the back of the group, sort of watching over the others. She is about 16 and has long, very blond hair and a classically beautiful face. She is silent, but her eyes are watching everything. She scratches her hands and her arms frequently, probably is nervous. Maybe she feels afraid.

Tom tried to sit next to her, but Bob tripped him as he was moving his chair.

Tom too, is very quiet and he doesn't seem to want to see very much. He looks down and pulls the loose thread on his sweater. Every once in a while Bobby takes a poke at him right in his arm. Tommy just keeps sitting there, very still. He is about 14 or 15 and still a "tow head."

Bobby is squirming in his chair and when not punching Tom he interrupts often, wanting to tell his own story. He doesn't have much patience. Bob wants us to know that he's mad, 'cuz dad hits him with a belt even when he didn't cause trouble. He says the teachers at school pick on him too. Nobody is listening. Bobby is 12. He has dark hair like Mom.

Sally sits slouched in her chair, chewing gum loudly. She swings her legs back and forth, back and forth, 'till Daddy tells her to stop. She gets mad at him. When the therapist asks her what she would like us to know, Sally beams and goes into a long story about how she is selling Girl Scout cookies all by herself. I think she is almost 10 years old.

The baby of the family is Karen (well until this new baby is born anyway, who is me). She is probably about five now. She likes to take care of our mom and she is handing her a tissue right now. Karen has pigtails and she seems really kind. She likes to wear skirts and she's going to start school soon. She doesn't talk much here in therapy.

Almost Real Family Sculpture #2

The occasion is a family meeting with the therapist right before Mom and Dad start their business, the J&E Laundry Mat. They are both optimistic these days with the possibility of a new life just ahead. They want to announce this to their children.

Betsy sits near her mother. She is all curled up in the chair and maybe inside herself too. She worries about the walk back and forth to school in this new neighborhood. She is thin, suffers from mononucleosis and generally is a sickly child. If it weren't for Mary Pat, her best friend in 5th grade, Betsy would be very lost. Her big sister Karen is like her mom and dad, both. She can go to her about anything and get help. Betsy silently strokes the soft gold velvet arm of the chair.

Karen goes to high school and wears a uniform. She even has a part time job at a custard stand. She talks to people a lot more now and even makes some jokes and laughs easily in this therapy session. She says she doesn't mind "watching out for" Betsy a lot, she knows mom is tired. Karen is excited about her new boyfriend and graduating soon. Karen and dad sing together into the tape recorder, sometimes. They get along really well. She sits near dad this time.

Sally is pregnant again. After she got married she had a "nervous breakdown" and had to be put in the hospital. In our family we don't talk about things like that but I know it was Grandpa's hospital, Saint Mary's. By now she has two little girls and a very nice businessman husband. They live in the suburbs. I visit sometimes and she teaches me how to clean. She is busy every single minute. I like being a part of her family. She says that she still cares about all of us. Maybe next summer I'll stay with her out at the lake. She said she'd teach me to swim if I help her take care of the children in the afternoons.

Bob moved away from the family and he lives out West somewhere, so we hardly ever hear from him. He married a woman and brought her home to live here, but then he was angry so much and too religious, so my mom and dad had him put into a mental hospital. That hurt his feelings deeply; now he felt even more misunderstood by the family and he went away and never came back. We heard he helped to raise his wife's first son and then they had their own baby, a little boy. Sometimes he writes us letters about Jesus.

Tom probably misses him. Now he is the only brother around. After the Navy he just had a very quiet life. Mom introduced him to one of the laundry customers because this woman had zip and mom thought Tom needed someone like that. After a while, they got engaged. Tom doesn't live with us but he comes over to visit a lot and to do his laundry. He doesn't talk in the therapy session.

Jane used to live with us in our last house in the back bedroom with her husband and their little boy. I played with him and pretended I was his big sister. Now she lives in Green Bay and they have another little boy. She isn't here today. Mom and Dad and I sometimes drive up there to visit them. Mom and I go in her car and Dad always goes alone because mom is afraid of his fast driving. Jane has a cozy house with her family.

It seems like Mom doesn't really like Dad very much but at the same time, she's trying to do everything "right" and be a good wife. Mom has something called scruples. She tells me often, to go to confession so my soul is clean. She works hard cleaning our house and cooking and she goes to church a lot. Mom mostly talks to the therapist this time. She tells him she is relieved that my dad is finally going to have his own business, doing work that he likes. She says she felt so guilty when he had to give up his dream in Arizona because of her being afraid of scorpions.

Dad talks a little bit this time, about how many jobs he's had and how he feels guilty because there was never enough money and his parents brought over food to us on the holidays. He still seems sad that we couldn't stay living in Arizona, where he had his new job. But he says that this is his second chance and he's ready to take the risk. He talks about his sports car too and his friends at The Stable. They all sing in barbershop quartets together. Then he smiles a real smile. I've never seen my dad this happy before. It's kinda weird.

There are only four of us in our house now. We are living behind the store in a big yellow house. I (of course you know that I am Betsy, don't you?) found a special room that is going to be my hiding place. It's way up in the attic, a room that has a door. I will keep my writing books up there and some water and my green wooden snake. I have to go up two flights of steps to get there and the attic door has a special key. No one else knows about my hiding place. It's quiet up there.

Almost Real Family Sculpture #3

Now there are just two of us in the family therapy session. Mom and I live in a little gray house on the East Side. I worry about her because she drinks so much brandy.

I watch her come home from her re-sale shop (she opened her own business with Grandma's money after Dad died) make supper, have a couple of drinks while she cooks and eats and then she just passes out on the couch. She doesn't seem to have much of a life. Going to church helps her. I have asked her to come with me today to therapy. She looks away from me often. I think she feels guilty.

I am 16 now and I am very unhappy. I'm failing at school, am worn out from my part time job and I am not liking my mom. I stay away from home as much as I can. I have changed my name to "Beth" because it's more mature. I'm dating a guy on the Marquette University track team. He and his team members live in a huge house about two blocks away. I've gone to bed with a couple of them; I don't know why. Usually it happens when I'm just hanging around waiting for my boy friend to come home and I'm drinking with them. I smoke cigarettes and try to act like everything is okay. I am very sad and lonely on the inside and I cry almost every day. Something is wrong with me, but I don't know what it is.

Maybe therapy will help. In the session, I sit way across the room from my mother and I share my worries about her with the therapist. He is very good looking and seems interested in listening to me. I begin to wear make up for our sessions. Soon the topic shifts to mostly me and I tell my mom she doesn't have to come with me anymore. This is the one thing in a week that I look forward to. The therapist and I sit closer together now. Someone is paying attention to me. I like it a lot.

Family

Family—the place we come from, the place we can never go back to and the people we carry inside with us, always and forever. As I age and mature, I am realizing more and more the power of the family.

I used to want to be a family therapist. I love facilitating groups and the family is absolutely the most interesting, complex and interwoven group of all. When I worked with families in crisis who would come in for counseling at the runaway shelter, I was humbled, inspired and amazed. The book *People Making* by Virginia Satir was required reading at the time and later in school, I discovered the wonderful book by the family therapist that took us through the whole process with one particular family. Later still, in my own recovery, there was *Another Chance* by Sharon Wegscheider-Cruise. I never pursued the final degree that I needed to work with families and sometimes I feel sad not to have been able to use myself in this way.

Family is so very important to me, personally. I have spent more than half my life being significantly influenced by the history I share with my family. I have been trying for over 40 years to unravel the mystery of my own past experiences. I will continue to be a product of my family in all those aspects of me that I like and am proud of, as well as those habit patterns that will continue to challenge me. Now, that is powerful.

I have lived, as well, in families that I have created. I did have some control over what I wanted these families to become. I gave birth to three children and we lived together with their father, later just us as a single parent family and then in a unit with my second husband. I have also lived as part of a couple where there were no children. In addition, I've lived in a small commune and I've made a sense of family with friends that I do not live with. My experiences in family, expectations and sense of values has changed over time.

Yet always there is the going back to this strong longing I have inside of me, for home and family. I think it's because my longing was never satisfied. I've not yet had enough, been fulfilled in this very important part of who I am, down deep inside me.

My Dad's Family, My Dad and Myself

Looking back, of course it's always so much easier to see where one has been, when one is past that point and everything that at one time had been hidden, becomes crystal clear. I know now how deeply affected I was by my father's death. He and I had never been close and out of that painful emptiness grew the bond I forged with him— the dream that one day we would be. I saw my dad as the sensitive, wronged, wounded soul that he was. His escape into mood music, classical and the requiems/his convertibles and fast sports cars/ his romantic escapades and abuse of alcohol—all of his hurts and how he coped with them, drew me to him. He needed my love and if given a chance, I was sure that I could help him feel better. Then maybe, he could love me back.

But we hardly knew each other, really. He had no idea that I, at age 14, was troubled and lonely, had no solid place to stand. I thought my mom was weak and naive, easy to fool. Yet her fears kept her anxiously on edge, and I had taken it on as my job to take care of her. So my sense of duty wed me to her when all I wanted to do was break away. I needed my dad to help me in doing that and he wasn't able to. I had just started high school when my dad suddenly went into the hospital and within several days he died.

It was a terrible shock to me, because I did not know that he was so sick, had been for months now. In our family we didn't talk about those things and how we were feeling about them. We didn't trust that we would be heard, responded to, as we needed to be. Much later in life, I was to learn that these were hallmarks of the dysfunctional family system: "Don't talk, Don't trust, Don't feel." So we all (six kids, mom and dad) just struggled along, each one of us so very alone.

My dad had been suffering with cancer for many months. Not even Mom knew until he became very ill. This was in the mid-fifties when everyone was terrified of cancer and there was no such tiling as successful treatment and "cure." We were told later that dad had been confiding in his dad, a general practitioner who sent him to one of his physician friends. Grandpa was heart broken because he had devoted his lifetime to healing and yet there was nothing he could do to help his own son.

This was Grandpa's eldest of eight (a previous child had died as an infant) and was to follow in his father's footsteps through private high school and college, then medical school and into the community in service. In fact, this is how mom and dad met; Dad was the teenage boy going on house calls with his dad, The Doctor, sitting behind the wheel in the model T Ford while he waited. Mom, a restless and an adventuresome young girl, enjoyed flirting with him in the driveway. They dated/ canoed on the Milwaukee river/ played tennis at Grandma Kane's house/danced in the third floor ballroom at the Roger's house. Dad, respectably Catholic, socially responsible and more than a little in love with his now pregnant Sweetheart, dropped out of school and "ran away" with Mom to be married. Soon there were more babies, one right after another.

I have very few memories of my father. Because I longed for his attention and love, each one has been of utmost importance to me. Yet the memories are like the black and white pictures I have, silent in their small golden frames. I remember there being almost no energy, feeling, life connection between us at all. Dad often slept in his big green chair in the living room. It was his place of escape. Sometimes he simply had his eyes closed and I'd tip toe around, not knowing if he was "here" or not. Other times I'd walk into a room and see him, eyes closed as well, grandly directing the symphony he was listening to on the radio.

Once early on a Saturday morning I walked through the store we owned, in front of where we lived, on my way to the basement. I was so scared to find a man sleeping on the floor of the store, more shocked to realize that it was my father. Later mom explained that she had locked him out of the house. It was late, he still wasn't home and she simply locked up. I used to wonder where he had been, out so late.

I remember being at The Stable, the bar in our neighborhood where dad had friends. I used to walk back and forth past it on my way to and home from school. Once, on a Sunday morning after church, he took my mom and me there with him. I played the bowling game that had a "puck" with it. I'd push real hard through some sawdust to get it to knock down the pins. I was impatient after a while; we had to stay there so long. I remember looking at my dad, sitting on a barstool, talking and laughing. These were the people he was in the choir and barbershop quartets with.

He loved singing and these were his friends. It was the only time I ever heard my dad laughing.

My dad taught me how to make scrambled eggs, moving them very gently so they would stay fluffy and light. Sometimes, when he'd iron his gray pants, always careful to get the seam exactly right in them with that damp kitchen towel laying under the iron, I'd hear him whistling a song. I must have been afraid of or for my dad, because I can remember now always being relieved at those times and I can almost feel again my shoulders dropping, "Oh good, he's happy."

My older sisters and brothers have told me that dad used to be angry with them often. He used to hit my brother (the bad one) with a belt. They told me Dad was often out of work, too. He had never really learned a skill or a trade, so the jobs open to him were all service positions that paid very little. For a while he drove a cab, emptied candy machines that my uncle had placed around town, got a "fireman's" license in order to ran the furnace and boiler at his father in-law's shoe factory. The must have felt defeated, his pride broken and bent after years of barely surviving. In those times, how a man provided for his family was his whole identity and Dad was never able to have the satisfaction of being able to do that without the help of his or Mom's parents. Of the extended family, Mom and Dad's brothers and sisters, there were attorneys, physicians and nurses, prominent businessmen and military leaders. We were the poor ones. Grandma and Grandpa Roger's used to leave baskets of food for us on the porch at Thanksgiving time, Christmas and Easter.

Always, I thought of myself as not having a family; no parents, no sisters, no brothers. I don't know if by some

The Crazy Quilt

memory of a past life or some half forgotten dream or simply because it sounds like my emotional story, but my frame of reference was life as a "street urchin" in the cobblestones of Old England; cold, wet, dirty, hungry, lonely, scared, desperate and being a "beggar child," barely surviving.

I cherish the few times of actual connection with my father. We drove to Arizona when I was 5; all of us kids in the car except my oldest sister, who had just gotten married. My dad was in charge. He knew where he was going (to a dream of his to start over with his family) and he knew how to get us all there with him (he kept maps and tabs of gasoline payments, on a gray metal clipboard under his arm). He felt hopeful and we all could feel it with him. I felt his strength, his ability to take care of me and I felt secure. That was "family" to me. Five of us kids in the car with Mom and Dad, driving mountain roads and sleeping in motels. I loved it. I felt alive and excited. I have a great picture of myself in bib overalls, sitting on a fence next to my dad and my brothers. I asked to have it taken. I wanted to remember that I was happy.

Another was when he held me on his lap and we made a recording of my voice, to send to "Billy The Brownie" on the radio. Then he recorded himself, telling me the beautiful Christmas Story. I was about 6. I still have that precious record he made for me with his own label, "Rogers Recording Service" on it. Now the sound is all scratchy, but I can still hear the tremor of my fathers' low and tender voice, telling me the story. I felt his love and I felt so very special. It was tangible and real and I had absolute trust in it.

Much later, when I was a young teenager, I realized that if I was going to have any further connection with my dad, I had to initiate it. At some inner level, I felt the urgency of it. I wanted so much to be close to my dad. He loved sports cars, had one and then another at this point in his midlife. He also had started his own business and while still the loner and recluse, I knew he felt better about himself. I remember taking photographs of him in or next to his cars, one with he and mom together. I asked to go with him to a race at Elkhart Lake and while I held my breath, he answered "yes." Maybe he knew the urgency, too. We had a beautiful, warm and sunny day together, the long ride and sitting on a blanket on a hill while we watched the race. We didn't talk much at all. We stopped on the way home and had supper in a smalltown pub along the way. It was awkward and yet I felt the moments hold us in a sense of timelessness. My dad and I were together. Nothing and no one could ever take that away. This was mine.

When I was five on our trip, my dad had seemed so competent, looking at maps, carrying that silver clipboard under his arm, later showing us Camel Back Mountain. He was never the same after we came back from Arizona. The family story was that he had to give up his dream because Mom couldn't stand living there with the bugs. I think my dad gave up a lot of his dreams. He didn't know how to go after them, make them real for himself. It was easier to blame Mom, marriage, family, being broke, being disheartened and in the end, being sick and dying, then it was to face the unknown and have courage enough to build a new life for himself. His romantic dream was always of being in Pongo Pongo, the South Sea island paradise. I'd like to believe that he finally found his way there.

The last time I saw my dad, he was dying. I knelt on the cold concrete floor of his room with my oldest brother, not knowing what was really going on or what it was I was supposed to be doing. Mom, Aunt Janet and I went down to the chapel and prayed. When we got back they told us Dad had died. It was a very formal funeral. Student nurses from St. Mary's, where Grandpa was Chief of Staff, formed an honorary guard outside of our church. They stood in two rows facing each other, their swords touching and navy blue capes with red linings blowing in the wind. All of them were dressed in white uniforms, caps, even white stockings and shoes. The scene was confusing and frightening to me.

Dad's coffin seemed very big. I had never seen one before. The procession of cars that followed us to the cemetery, all with black flags on their antennas, was long. We talked very little on the way. The last thing I remember was seeing all of us dressed in black, standing near to Dad's coffin in that pure, white expanse of snow. The snow was falling lightly and the grass had all been covered. It was very beautiful to experience—the gray skies, the wet, black trees, the gray stone markers of all different sizes reaching up out of the earth. After a while, we quietly turned and walked away. I was numb for months. In fact, my trust in life was not the same for a very long time. My father had died and I still needed him.

Looking back over my father's lifetime with what I know now, I'm sure that he himself suffered from deep depression as far back as his youth. In all of the photographs I've seen of him as a young man and as a child, he is very serious. Mom told me that he felt the weight of responsibility for his younger brothers and sisters, quite heavily. Dad's birth, after the death of the first son, probably led to him to trying to make up for that loss by always doing his best. Both his parents were very involved in community service, their social obligations and the story goes, in their riveting relationship with each other. The seven children huddled together, befriending and watching out for one another, in what may have otherwise been a lonely household for just one or two of them.

Except for Amelia. She was not only the live-in housekeeper and cook, but also the children's caretaker, confident and ally as well. In every holiday gathering, her presence was as an important member of the family. There was an old home movie of Thanksgiving day, that became a hilarious legend: (played backward) Amelia's taking the oval platter, with it's golden brown turkey, up off the dinning room table and walking proudly back through the swinging door with it to the kitchen, while the family watched helplessly.

The three story, corner house they lived in on Milwaukee's fashionable East Side, years later became the site of a residential treatment center. In my early 40's, while back in school earning a degree in Alcohol and Other Drug Abuse counseling, I did a field placement semester in exactly the same house. The second floor meeting room with the fireplace had been Grandma and Grandpa's bedroom, Mom told me. As I ran up the narrow back stairway, I thought of my dad and aunts and uncles having run up these same steps as children. The third floor, now mostly executive offices and the library that I was in charge of, had been a huge ballroom. Mom and Dad had attended many formal affairs with string quartets there, as Grandma and Grandpa entertained.

My Grandma Rogers was an ominous figure to me. She was tall and big boned and seemed very strong-minded. She had bowling trophies on the mantel (as a child, I never knew until then that women bowled) and was nothing like I thought a grandma should be. In fact, she even drank "cocktails" with her husband every night before dinner, often laughed, had a loud voice and seemed very sure of herself. I felt afraid of her. It was Grandpa Rogers who was the heart of the family. He was short and round and always seemed to have a twinkle in his eye. He always seemed magical to me. Because of his commitment to be of service to the poor in his neighborhood, he became affectionately known as "the Doctor of Cherry Street." I liked him very much, but I was a little afraid of him too. Maybe because both of my parents wanted to please them, therefore proving that they were "acceptable," I grew up aware that my paternal grandparents had a tremendous amount of power.

They did have money, old money, and that was intimidating. They owned the little cottage at Lake DeNoon that we stayed in for two weeks during the summers. Theirs was called "the big house" up on the hill. Grandpa had a beautiful, light golden brown horse named Dixie, and he rode every day in the late afternoon. Dixie was a Tennessee Walker and she had a slow, rhythmic gait. I'd see Grandpa off in the distance, sitting proud on his beloved Dixie, and I'd hear him whistling some song, loud and clearly. Often on weekends Grandma and Grandpa would have parties down by the fireplace/grill and it's circular stone wall. Nurses and nuns, priests and young interns from the hospital would be sitting around in lawn chairs. There was always a lot of visiting and eating, drinking and singing. We had a lot of family songs, some in German and toasts and "bravo's." Everyone seemed to love my Grandpa and Grandma Rogers.

My Aunt Rosemary, one of Dad's sisters, was a nurse and worked in Grandpa's office on 3rd Street. I remember going there on the bus with my mom and sometimes we would stop at Schuster's across the street to buy take-home delicatessen food for our supper. After a while I learned the bus route and felt proud to be able to go by myself. Rosalie would have her starched white uniform and cap on and I would get my weekly "iron shots" for the anemia after I had mononucleosis. Sometimes she'd ask if I wanted to go in and say hi to Grandpa. He'd be at his big office desk (that later I took into my home as a proud link to our history) and he'd ask me how I was feeling, ask if I was getting stronger and sometimes he'd listen to my heart with the stethoscope he had hung around his neck. He was always so kind to me. Rosalie and my mom were close friends and dear confidants all through the years. I loved and honored my Grandpa. His spirit is close to me, still.

My Mom's Family, My Mom and Myself

Mom was afraid of her influential in-laws and I'm sure that's what kept most of us kids from really getting to know them, or at least never feeling at ease around them. To Mom, they seemed disapproving of her. I think most of it was Mom's own guilt and probably what she took on from my dad as his guilt and shame too, in not following in his father's footsteps. In those days of course, pregnancy outside of wedlock was all "hush, hush" and a situation that not only brought shame on the family in eyes of the community, but "forced" too many young men and women like my parents into "an acceptable marriage."

I don't know if Mom's own parents ever knew the truth about the "hurry" they were in to get married. By now, my Grandpa and Grandma Casting were used to their headstrong daughter's ways. As a teenager at the German and English Academy, Mom had been reprimanded for taking her girlfriends to The Milwaukee Athletic Club restaurant, ordering ice cream sodas all around and casually putting it on the bill of her father. She'd bounce a basketball in "tomboy" style all the way home from school, swim out to the raft with her pack of forbidden cigarettes raised high in the air, waltz out of the house on a date wearing her snooty sister's new mohair sweater.

Yet her dad had a soft spot for this fourth child and his scoldings were gentle and quickly forgotten, as he asked her to play the piano for him in the evening. Often he'd bring back surprises for the children from various business trips and his homecomings were always special occasions. Later in the family there were hushed whispers about his money, his women and his whisky. He suffered huge financial losses during the depression and died early, of a "liver disease." I never knew my Grandpa Casting. I think that most likely he was loud, a thick cigar sticking out of his mouth, grandiose about his wealth and importance and died early because of the heavy drinking that he did, especially after losing several of his big business holdings.

My Grandma Casting was the mild mannered one in this family. She was small, delicate with her long hair coiled primly at the back of her neck. Grandma painted china with small flowers, one of the talents of the Ladies of her day. She loved to plan meals with her cook (Grandma was an early nutritionist, a follower of Adel Davis) and took pride in setting a beautiful long table for family dinners, when her husband was home. Over the years, Grandma developed a "nervous condition" that kept her most often secluded in her upstairs bedroom suite. She was "ill" for seven years. I have come to understand that this must have been an early "nervous breakdown" and of so much personal shame at that time, that the "stricken" just hid away, resting and taking tonic of cod liver oil, to build themselves up again. This kind of "nervous disease" was kept secret at the time, by my relatives as well as by other families who could afford to hire live in help. I remember my Grandma in later years, during the times that she would take the streetcar over to our house, always carrying a shopping bag with her, full of oranges and vitamins for us kids. I thought she was most wonderful and dear.

Grandma herself had grown up in a genteel social class. In her youth she and her sister (they were named Onalie, the Native American name of my grandmother, and Analie) were of course exposed to the arts and travel through Europe. Grandma painted and I have some of her watercolors hanging in my home today. Her parents had a home built on their estate, for her wedding gift. It was a squarish gray stone house with green shutters, up the hill from the Milwaukee River and it was there that my mom spent all of her growing up years. My mother grew up with gardens and swimming lessons and going to the theater. Her maternal grandparents lived just down the way. Mom would tell us about the Christmas tree there, with small glowing candles on all the branches and about listening to the glockenspiel tinkling as it turned slowly around and around.

My mom also had some traumatic experiences as a child. She had accidentally been trapped in the attic one day, calling out the window for a long time, "Somebody help me, I'm locked in the attic!" Nobody heard her. Mom developed a lifelong panic disorder that she linked to that experience. She was extremely claustrophobic and it took all the courage she had to ride in an elevator "that might get stuck between floors." At one very stressful point in her life, she became so agoraphobic that she was not able to leave the house for seven long years. The older children went to the grocery store; she had things delivered. As a child, my mom was also sexually exploited down in a dark corner of the cellar one-day, when the gardener exposed himself to her and invited her to come and touch him. She was terrified. She felt ashamed. I don't think that she ever told anyone else in her family. I feel very sad that mom was never offered any help in learning how to deal with these things that left her feeling so powerless and afraid.

In honor of one of her birthdays, Mom took some of us, now adult children, on a tour of her family home. It was wonderful to see the inside of this place that had held so many memories for my mother. Her sister Jane, the Aunt I was closest to on mom's side of the family, came along and it was fun to hear them reminisce together about their childhood. They talked about finding their Easter baskets out on the front lawn in the morning, running down the hill on a summer afternoon to go swimming in the river, walking over to their Grandma Kane's house to play tennis on the court. Mom seemed to have an enchanted childhood, even the magic of a girl and boy twin in her family, but her stories often had great overtones of loneliness to them. She showed us the green ceramic tiles around the fireplace and the corner she used to sit in, lonely, to read cherished childhood books. I understood better now, how she'd been referred to in our family as "the poor little rich girl."

In spite of the frailty of her mother, my mom always seemed to have a mixture of awe, respect for and fear of her authority. Even in Grandma's last years, when she was confined to bed and Mom moved into her little apartment in order to take care of her, Grandma ruled the roost. She instructed Mom as to what to buy at the grocery store, how to cook their supper and even scolded into the kitchen one night, as she heard mom making an ice cream sundae, "That's not good for you." Grandma was the practical one, her husband the wild romantic. I can understand Mom's need in her life to rebel, as well as to seek out her father's attention. Grandma was stern.

Yet, of all my grandparents, it was Grandma Casting that I knew and loved the best. In her later years, she grew strong and capable, learning how to manage by herself and handle her late husband's investments. I remember her showing up at our side door often, with a brown shopping bag full of delicatessen food from Schuster's; bananas, vitamins and cod liver oil for me. Grandma always wore her little black hat with the delicate netting on top. I was fascinated with her fox fur, each of their mouths biting onto the tails of the one ahead of it, their little beady glass eyes. It was Grandma who made sure we all had good shoes from her factory and of course fruit (which we couldn't afford) like Adel Davis, the nutritional expert of the day instructed.

It was Grandma who paid the dressmaker to make my very own white satin ballerina costume and took me to buy my white satin toe dancing shoes for my 11th birthday. It was Grandma, I learned later, who was standing at the stove cooking oatmeal for breakfast, her hat on her head, when Dad got home from the hospital and announced that everyone had a new baby sister and that her name would be Elizabeth. Grandma always helped take care of all of us, and I very quietly loved her with all of my heart.

I keep an oil painting that my Grandma Casting did, framed in black wood, hanging in my living room. Next to it is her picture as a young woman. I also have a picture of her sister, my Aunt Analie, as she graduated from college. They are lovely studio portraits, of two very different sisters. I have a big, black straw hat hanging nearby that belonged to my Aunt Analie and that I rescued from her estate sale. The lives of these two siblings fascinate me. Onalie, a very traditional wife and mother, suffered a nervous breakdown that must have resulted in terrible isolation and shame. Analie, a well educated, single woman (most unusual at that time) traveled to Europe with friends and became a political radical, proficient in public speaking and persuasion.

They both speak to me out of the stories of the past. The family property, where they grew up along the river, was donated to the Friends Meeting Society by Aunt Analie (great aunt really) shortly before she died. It now is cherished and cared for by the Quakers who have made a nature preserve of it, that protects and nurtures the very same trees and has been replanted with the same native plants that my grandma and my mother after her, grew up with. This is where we scattered my mother's ashes, respectfully bringing her full circle, back home again.

Back in the days when my mother and father began their "courting" it was actually right under the respective families' noses. Soon they began dating in groups of friends and alone; canoeing on the Milwaukee River, swimming, laughing and singing, Dad playing his harmonica, playing tennis in doubles and necking in the dark in Dad's fathers' car. They were madly in love. Then, they were expecting a baby.

I believe that for Mom and Dad this was a wonderful opportunity to do what they really wanted to do anyway, which was to rebel against the tight constraints of their respective families and run away to get married. They started a whole new life for themselves, as sweethearts together.

Most of us children experienced that romance, along with the later angers, silences and betrayals. Mom left us many of the anguished pieces of poetry she wrote late at night, alone at the kitchen table. It was very confusing to us, their children, to experience one thing going on and to be told something else was happening instead. Yet we held to their illusion, passed down to us, because they wanted us to. We all remember hearing Mom and Dad singing together, seeing them holding hands, smiling into each other's eyes and harmonizing for us on their song, "Side by Side". We sing their song still in our family reunions.

My Family and I

I was the youngest child of six and had a troubling relationship with Mom and Dad from the very start. I was conceived just as Dad was about to leave for Alaska and long term work on the pipeline being built there. It was at the beginning of the 40's, the aftermath of the 2nd. World War years and in a very strained economy. I believe that secretly in my fathers' heart he was looking foreword to getting away. My mother panicked at the prospect of being left alone with five children and little money. Then suddenly after six years, she was pregnant again. Dad stayed home. From my youngest years on, I've had a grave sense of responsibility for everyone I was close to. I thought that my job was to save them, as it had been to save my parents and their marriage.

Most of my life, I tried to take care of my mother. During a long course of my therapy, the emphasis was on separating from the symbiotic relationship I'd built with my mother and being nurtured by "the giving mother," my therapist, (who would allow me to curl up on pillows in her arms, as she held me with love). I found out that probably as early as during my first few months in the world, I "turned off" my needs such as crying when I was hungry and needed to be fed. Inez, my therapist at the time, thought I was learning even that early, that what I wanted I couldn't get (carried over into my adult pattern of subjugating my wants and needs to those of my intimate others). My mother's needs were big, urgent and they were the ones that counted. After all, it was Mom that we all revolved around and if she wasn't ok we weren't going to be either.

Mom did a lot of hemorrhaging after I was born and was confined to her bed for long periods of time. When the "new baby" wasn't being brought to her, my primary care was being provided by my two older sisters. Inez helped me understand that at ages 6 and 10, they were not capable of providing for my needs, in spite of the fact that they wanted to be. Even today, they brag with how it was them who took care of me. It is their way of saying to me, "This is how much we loved you," in response to my willingness to talk about how I did not feel loved as a child. They are trying to help me, I know. They don't seem able to understand how it was for me, not to have had a mother (even though they too, must have suffered that loss).

I remember how shocked I was when my therapist introduced the idea that as a child, I had been abused. At the time I was working with teenage runaways and I knew very well what parental abuse looked like. I had never been burned with cigarettes, locked in a closet or beaten with a coat hanger. Then I found out that "neglect" is another form of abuse. I was horrified, yet I felt the truth of it. I wanted very much to protect the image I had of my parents, especially of my mother. I wanted equally to uncover the beginnings of current self neglect and abuse. To do that, I needed to understand the origins of my behavior. That meant being brave enough to look back at my childhood. After a lot of denial, a lot of resistance, I was able to do that.

I grew up feeling very lonely. My sister Karen was a godsend to me. She and Mary (her friend from down the block) would do the dishes together and sing in beautiful harmony. They laughed a lot and sometimes took me with them to the drugstore, where we sat on red and silver stools and drank cherry cokes at the long counter. Theirs was the only "sunshine" in my life. I hated school; I had a very hard time concentrating and now, would be labeled ADD and probably get some help. But at the time, I just felt "dumb" and often was humiliated when I'd be called on to stand at the board and do math problems or remain standing next to my desk because I'd be one of the failures in the spelling quiz. Often, I pretended to be sick so I could stay at home and not have to be in that stressful setting. I slid by with barely passable grades. I don't remember either parent ever asking me if I had homework to do, or looking at my report card.

Mary Pat and Peggy were my first friends. Peggy was quiet and little, like me. I was fascinated with her dark hair and big brown eyes. In my family most of us had blond hair and hazel eyes. Peggy and I would tell each other our secrets and that sure felt good to be so safe with another person. When I had to move away from Peggy's neighborhood, I thought my heart would break, but we found out we could visit each other's houses and still play together. We used to pretend we were a family, had a baby and all. I was the dad and had a special hat with a visor that I liked to wear.

I liked Mary Pat because she was fat (we were all pretty thin in my family) and very bossy. She would get me to do all sorts of daring things that we weren't supposed to do, like climbing up the back of billboards and sitting right on the edge on top. We would go up into my attic and while leaning out the window, drop ice cubes right in front of (or on the head of) the customers coming into our store and then when they were startled, we would laugh and laugh. When I stayed overnight at Mary Pat's house, we would sleep in her mother's double bed. Sometimes she would lay on top of me and pretend she was my husband. I was always afraid her mother would come in right then, but she never did.

I wanted and I needed to be loved. From very early on, I realized that I could not get that love from my mother, who was totally engaged with just trying to survive her own psychological torment and unable to nurture me. So I found my place by becoming "the good girl." I kept quiet. I did not make demands on her. I tried to figure things out for myself. I kept the peace. I pretended that I was doing okay so she wouldn't have to "worry" about me. Even before that, I silently agreed to all the limitations she placed on me, trying to keep me "safe" by projecting her own fears about the world around her, onto me. Mom kept me tied to her in this way. As she was, I was afraid of just about everything "out there" and it was a handicap as real as any that might have been visible to others. I gave up my natural curiosity to explore and my inherent life energy to create. In my fierce loyalty, I became "like her" so that she would not feel threatened by me.

Eventually, I insured myself another important place in her world. I became "the mother" who nurtured the lost child in her. I listened, understood, empathized, supported and helped her make decisions. I was the one who kept order in our home. I cleaned the house, did the dishes, made sure the doors were locked at night. I encouraged and soothed her when she felt afraid. I pretended not to notice how she'd burn something in the frying pan, leave things around the house in such a chaotic mess, and pass out on the couch as she watched TV in the evening. We'd go to church together on Sundays and stop at the corner bakery for hot ham and potato rolls. I just wanted to be "normal" and have a mom who knew how to take care of me. I thought that if I took very good care of her, then maybe she would be able to. I prayed that she would change. I prayed a lot in those days.

It was around then, that I noticed my mother's drinking. We always had a liquor cabinet in the house and my dad had often come home very late and, I think, drunk after his frequent nights out, but I just had not seen my mother drinking. Maybe I was noticing it now that she was even more alone and I was increasingly aware of that burden on me. I had just discovered boys and loud music and dancing and even using alcohol myself to numb the pain. I used to save peanut butter jars and slowly fill them from my mother's supply, after she was sleeping. The Saturday night parties in somebody's basement were always such a tremendous relief. It didn't take long to find out about sex and what a powerful bargaining tool it was. More than anything, I wanted a boyfriend to love me. I would take care of him in return. From everything I read and heard and saw this was the thing that would give my life meaning. It would be easy for me.

I learned to drive and was the only one of my girlfriends who had access to their parent's car, so I felt really important. I perfected driving with one hand, holding a cigarette in the other, a can of beer between my legs and calling out the window to the guys next to us at the red light, "Hey, you wanna drag?" Wisconsin Avenue, between 27th Street and the old train depot at the lakefront, was my territory. As I became more sophisticated, my "hang outs" became dark and smoky "coffee houses" on the East Side, where I began to search for myself through bongo drums and poetry. Always, there was a long trail of boys and young men traveling through my life. I tried to hold onto them. I gave them everything they wanted. There was one for three years while I was in high school. He was older, tall, very charming, demanding, controlling, aggressive, dangerous. He taunted and belittled me. I was wildly in love with him. He stood me up one last time, a date I had really looked forward to. I was hurt enough to finally break up with him. On Sunday afternoons I used to sit on a bench on top of the hill near the tennis court, watching couples walking by, hand in hand. I was so lonely and so filled with despair, I'd ask God to please let me die so I wouldn't have to go through this awful pain anymore. I was 17.

What I didn't know at the time, nor did anyone else who was trying to help me (my mom, my sister Karen and my best friend Serena) was that I was experiencing serious depression. I had moved out on my own in my junior year of high school and was living with three girls my age in an apartment. I wasn't eating right, if at all (that was one of the nurturing ways my mom was there for me earlier and I think that refusing to eat like she would want me to was another way to say "I don't need you anymore"). I stayed up late visiting with roommates or writing poetry and got up early to get to school and then my part time job as a "nurses aid." It was very stressful. I worked in pediatrics and then in the three bed burn unit. Since it was the only burn unit in the city we got all the extremely serious cases and I took my role as medical support person very seriously. On my free weekends I did a lot of drinking and was sexually seductive and desperately indiscriminate. I hardly had time to feel how really lost and lonely I was inside.

I graduated by the skin of my teeth (always the "bad" student, absent too much/not able to concentrate and retain/ always trying to catch up from behind). I hated school, was so relieved when it was over. All I cared about was finding someone to love me. The only thing that helped me have any understanding of myself/of life that was larger than my own, was the comfort that I found in poetry. Thanks to my senior English teacher (who told my mom that I was 'a dear,' that she wanted to put me in her sleeve and take me home). When Mom told me, I was so surprised that someone cared about me. Reading and writing became my lifelines. There were others like me and they had survived and even made sense out of this all. Maybe it was possible that I could, too.

At 17 I moved out, finishing high school while living in an apartment with three other girls who needed to be separate from their families too. It was a relief to be away from the disappointment and caretaking responsibility of Mom, but I felt guilty about leaving her all alone. Within a year after graduation, I was having what I know now to be my first "nervous breakdown." I'd thought I might be pregnant, my casual boyfriend refused to be involved. I was working nights dealing with death and loss constantly. I was terribly over tired and undernourished and I couldn't stop crying. Mom was scared for me. She sold her mother's heirloom china, got money together for me to take a Greyhound bus and made arrangements with an old friend for me to visit with her on the West Coast.

I quit my job, moved out of my apartment, and took the emergency trip to "save me" and proceeded to pick up a sailor on the bus, somewhere around Tulsa, Oklahoma. After a day or two of traveling together, I proposed the idea of marriage to him in a roundabout, joking way. He accepted. Within that next year we were walking down a sacred church aisle after vows that we, as a young and naive couple who were searching for love, took to heart most sincerely. I was so happy and well on my way to a new life where I believed I wouldn't hurt anymore. It was only then, from the safety of the East Coast where I lived with him, that I was able to start a new relationship with my mother. I had really broken away this time and she had survived it. Finally, I could breathe my own breaths.

All through the seven years of my marriage, the birth of my three children and my husband's various jobs that kept us moving back and forth between Wisconsin and Ohio, my mother was my confidant and friend. My best friend, actually. She and my sisters were constant sources of support, through the many letters we all sent back and forth in the mail and the occasional, very expensive phone calls. We visited. Mom saw me through all of my periods of deep and debilitating depression. I felt her fierce loyalty and her deep love of me like I had never felt it before.

Mom made many adjustments in her own life, to help me take care of my children after my divorce. Often she was the other parent, taking my children in on weekends so that I could work or have a break. She was the one who celebrated with me, all of their small successes. She was the one person I could count on to listen to me, to know me, to truly care. It was during this time, that I began to notice my mother's strengths. I realized that she was very resourceful. She had married again, a childhood sweetheart who longed for her companionship. As he generously shared what he had, it gave Mom some "time out" from her struggles financially and was a chance for her to rest. She was able to take better care of herself now and she had energy left over for me. She was always steady in crisis (her whole life a training ground). For the first time, I could lean on her. For the first time, I could be the one who was the child.

Over the years after her husband died, our love and friendship continued to deepen. I had done the work in therapy to separate from her and was no longer bound to her out of the old sense of "obligation." I had become stronger, too, and I wanted to give to my mom. We talked on the phone; she'd call to tell me if something good was on TV or ask how my writing was going. My mom was a writer too and I began to collect her work to pass on to the family. I'd go over on Fridays, twice a month and clean for her, and do her grocery shopping. I'd be scrubbing the toilette and she'd be calling to me to come into the living room and visit with her. Soon I started coming by every week, calling her more often, just to check that she was okay. I saw my mother aging, forgetting things, losing her balance, sleeping and isolating more, eating less. I'd sit on the toilette with the top down, while she took a shower every week or so, in case she'd fall. She'd send me home with a bag of groceries and slip me a twenty-dollar bill. I'd stand at the bus stop, late on a Friday night and feel tired yet full.

I was Mom's primary caretaker. It was assumed that since I was in town and after the children left I had no family to take care of, this would be the arrangement. Besides, by unspoken agreement among my three sisters, "Wasn't it only right that I should be paying mom back for all her help to me physically, emotionally and financially, when I was so down?" It was a role reversal I knew only too well with her. I slipped easily back into the nurturing parent role and she once again, could depend on me, like the fragile, scared child that she was. I felt angry with my sisters and brothers that they chose to be so loosely involved in my mother's life at this point. This time though, I did not feel resentful of Mom herself. A part of our life was honest and true. She was my aging mom, who lived alone and needed my help, and I was the grownup who loved her and this time wanted to give it.

Within time, Mom's increasingly limited mobility and pain of osteoporosis demanded a long hospital stay that was resolved with my sister Sally's and my decision to place Mom in a nursing home. It was obvious to me, as well as to the rest of the family through me, that Mom needed supervised care, safety, companionship and ongoing medical help, yet it was one of the most difficult decisions I've ever had to make. I felt so helpless. There were simply not any other possibilities. I felt the deep guilt and shame of "abandoning" her just when she needed me most. After the decision and transfer was finally made, I was also relieved. Now Mom would be taken care of and I wouldn't have to try to do it all.

It turned out that these last six years or so of Mom's life were relatively easy for her and allowed me freedom, in which I had renewed ability to be there for her in a loving and committed way. For the first time since early childhood, all Moms' needs were being taken care of and she loved the attention. For the first time, Mom had the help of medication for her anxiety and for her depression. For the first time in her adult life, Mom was relaxed without the use and abuse of alcohol.

After many long years of being worn out from the constant crisis of simply trying to survive, Mom began to enjoy things again. I'd take her out into the side yard in her wheelchair and we'd sit in the sunshine, Mom closing her eyes and turning her face up to the warmth. She looked forward to her meals in the dining room, that little bit of sociability, another patient playing the piano after dinner. I used to try to find cards for her, with pictures of rabbits on them. When she was a little girl, she was fascinated with seeing little brown rabbits jump up out of the wildflowers and run across the prairie next to her house. There was an innocent kind of magic in that for her, as held in many of her memories of an easier time.

I'd read the letters from grandchildren to her, that she'd proudly show me as soon as I arrived. Mom would tell me about the visits of kind social workers and later introduce me to them. I told her my stories and she listened with such compassion and always encouragement. We had precious hours together. I'd bring children's books with bright pictures from the childcare center where I worked, and we'd look at the pictures together. Sometimes we just sat quietly and held hands.

Yet it was hard going home so late on the bus night after night in the snow, after a busy workweek. I got very weary of it. I was angry with my sisters and brothers. I felt sad and alone; looking for the quilt my daughter knit for her, lost somewhere down in the laundry room/ hearing Mom tell me how she'd call out for help, over and over, and nobody came/ walking in one afternoon to find Mom slumped over in her chair, drooling, a puddle on the floor. I was shocked, scared and eventually furious when I realized that an inattentive staff was overmedicating her. There was the hostile roommate she was afraid of. There were the ones who died right next to her and Mom just had to get used to it. There was the serious infection she got in the hospital and was in isolation from. My sister and daughter and I prayed over her as she was dying from it and then she recovered. I often felt angry and helpless, dependent myself on the skills and compassion of the staff, yet grateful to them at the same time for doing the job that I couldn't do.

One rainy August night, as I got up to go to the bathroom, I saw my telephone answering machine blinking in the dark. The nursing home had called at 2:30 am and when I called them back I found out that my mom had died peacefully in her sleep just a short time before. No one had realized how serious her chest cold had been, except maybe my older sister who had just been in town to spend two weeks with Mom. Jane told me later how strange it was to be hearing herself giving Mom, on that last day, permission to leave us whenever Mom felt she was ready to die. It was no coincidence, we are sure. Mom needed to know that all her children could get along without her, especially this firstborn, emotionally connected with Mom like I had been. It was exactly this willingness to let her go that Mom was able to gracefully receive.

I was honored to have my family agree to allow me to plan and facilitate Mom's memorial service. It was my last gift to Mom. Including my older sister Karen, we established a ritual that was spiritually comforting to so many of us with different belief systems. We all gathered at the Quaker Meeting house, on the land my mom had grown up on. In silent procession, we walked the path through the trees and down to the river. We scattered her ashes there. Later we looked at family photographs and held Mom's treasured household things, her special antiques and her beautiful poetry. We told the well-worn stories and we sang the familiar songs. We shared food and we laughed and we cried. Mom would have loved it.

Chapter Four

Liz

By now all the leaves have fallen or been blown off the trees. Black branches are looking stark against the dark gray sky. It is late afternoon on Thanksgiving ay and I have this and one more glorious day to be home, free from any demands on me. The fresh air feels cool and I welcome it after holing up in my hot little apartment. I am noticing how few lights are on behind all these windows. Neighbors must be visiting family and friends who have big homes, invite everyone over to sit at long tables covered with white cloths. I'm glad to be alone today and yet I feel lonely.

One of the things I'm realizing at this point in my life is that I'm very worn out. I'm not pushing myself so hard and have less and less need for anyone else's approval. I am very content in the quiet around me, empty hours, and the opportunity to go inside and regenerate. I was telling Jeffrey just last week and Loretta the day before yesterday, how I've lost my confidence since I've been "back in." For a long time now I've taken for granted that I could cope with anything, had the skills, had the internal balance, had the support network in place. All I had to do was just keep pushing on. I found out last spring that it just isn't so.

Part I

It was early March and I was falling apart again. Standing at the window that first night in the white silky pajamas they gave me, I listened to the rain and started to cry. I was finally safe enough to let down my guard against the fear that once I started I might not be able to stop.

The day before I'd been in the last few minutes of a therapy session during an unusually long time of silence. I'd broken through, "Jeffrey, help me not kill myself." "Do you want to kill yourself Elizabeth? Do you know how to make a call to the emergency phone line in case you want help getting into a hospital? Do you want to be in the hospital? Do you want me to help you get into the hospital?"

I said "yes." I gave in. I felt relieved to give in. I gave up being so staunchly alone and I gave up my pride, however falsely I believed it acted as protection. I even gave up my being scared to give up, very slowly waving my small white flag of surrender. Jeffrey's voice is behind me on the phone, giving his credentials, office address and name of client. I asked him if he would hold hands with me while we waited for the police to arrive. I remember how big his hand was, wrapped around mine.

I knew, now almost forty years since I'd been locked up on psychiatric wards that I needed to go back in. It was almost like I had to. Not "had to" as if by anyone else's power or control, no. It was more by my own hand, as if simply the next thing to do. It was important to go back over some of the same places, see the pattern in terms of the whole "spiral" thing. It had been an overlapping of situations and of feelings that went deep and need to come up. I'd been scared, wanting for safe places and safe people to tell my stories to.

"Now" had become "then" a lot in the past month or two, as I'd decided to delve into the past. I was choosing to end an intimate relationship right then as well. As I started to look at my decisions and what I wanted, I began to see that all the significant relationships in my life had been built on allowing myself to be used and abused. None of my real need for attention in kind, loving, accepting, understanding, supportive, appreciative ways, had ever been met (other than in platonic friendships, maternal bonds or therapeutic relationships).

Journal entry-Thursday, March 9th, 2000

It's Thursday morning and I'm sitting in this big, empty room, on unit 43C at Milwaukee County Mental Health Hospital.

Because of this muscle relaxant, I'm feeling pretty "doped up" and it feels real good. But last night after taking the sleeping medication, I could hardly walk. It's been such a relief to be drugged after all this obsessive thinking and feeling, being aware of the need to act, not being able to decide which action to take.

My antidepressant has been increased. I'm not sure if I like that. More in the morning makes me more groggy. I've decided to refuse the muscle relaxant 3x's a day as it's ordered. It's just too much. Today my big thrill is to take a shower and wash my hair. I am looking forward to it.

The essence of all this is structure; regular sleep, food three times a day, even the social aspect (different from isolating myself like I do at home), is all helping me feel more grounded, back in my body. I felt good walking, walking, walking up and down the halls on the ward last night. "Crazy" as this sounds, I like being here. I feel secure.

Because I was brought in by police, there is a hearing on Monday morning. A lawyer saw me yesterday to let me know my rights. I wanted to ask him to repeat and to explain further but I felt foolish for not understanding, so I just nodded him away.

Today I was assigned to and met, a state public defender. She is clear and strong and I like her. Her job is to protect my interests so that I cannot be committed here for an indefinite period of time.

I asked my Doctor today, to suspend the suicide watch I'm on. He said they'd go down a notch till tomorrow, when the weekend psychiatrist would ask me how I was doing.

It's becoming real clear to me that my core issues are about lack of self-love. Dr. Schuster suggests I continue to work on that in therapy and that I get a sponsor in my CoDA program (Co-Dependents Anonymous) as a way to practice asking for and reaching out for help. "This is something you don't do very much of, isn't that right?" How does he know? He suggests that taking care of myself come first now, that later I can put energy into taking care of this relationship.

It's Saturday morning. I've just asked them to unlock this little sitting room (it's called the music room, they tell me). Sunshine is pouring in these big bay windows. This is the first time the sun has been shining in days.

This is the same room I sat in, had my first session in with the treatment team on Thursday. That day I talked about wanting to tear down all the draperies, wanting some outlet for this anger. I talked about wanting to kill myself but not wanting to traumatize my daughter, (saying that the other two who live away would feel sad, but would be better able to go on because of having more emotional distance).

I don't feel like hurting myself anymore. I like myself again. Last night for a few minuets, I actually felt happy and good with me. I started to feel like I had some energy, wanted to and could accomplish something.

This morning I was able to put on clean clothes. Terri brought me some T shirts and socks and underwear pants. Feels good just to be clean again. I'm looking forward to cutting my fingernails, tweezing my eyebrows. Oh the simple, simple things about being free.

It's very strange to me to be locked up like this (even my own bathroom door locked, my dresser and my closet) and not mind it. In fact, I feel very safe here. I'm off the suicide watch as of 3:00 PM today. As of this afternoon, I have my shoelaces back.

Journal entry-Sunday, March 12th, 2000

I'm feeling so much better. I feel alive again, have some energy. Found a picture of a butterfly in the newspaper—transformation. I'm not angry anymore, at myself / with anyone else. I sat in the music room just now and someone was playing a tape of gospel music. Uplifting. I've been praying, just wanting the presence of my spirit helpers around me. The stones in my pocket that Terri gave me feel grounding and good. The book she brought, Step Back From the Exit, is validating my reality in a way that no staff person here is and this is helping me a lot.

I called Charlie today to say I was here. We talked a little and it felt good until she called me a "therapy addict." Any name-calling is cruel and this feels especially mean because my therapy with Jeffrey has been life saving to me. Wish I had said, "Well, I am an addict, but therapy isn't one of my addictions. Staying with people who put me down, judge and then reject me is and has been. I am recovering now. I'm learning how to detach from the sting of a comment like that (feels like being slapped) and how to use that as a signal that I'm being verbally abused."

It's this kind of thing that brings me to wanting to end the relationship. Charlie's lack of understanding, loving and respecting me hurts. This makes me think it's not a safe or supportive atmosphere I'm in as we do therapy together. I don't feel safe being intimate with someone who devalues this important process I'm involved in, the soul healing work that I'm doing.

Terri just came for a short visit on her way to listen to the singing crystal bowls. I was able to tell her about my experience on the phone and she was able to help me see that this is about power and control. I told Terri that I had gone way past my limits in giving of myself to Charlie and that I was at the point of just calling it quits. Terri reminds me, "You don't want to lose yourself, especially to someone who doesn't value you." It was so affirming.

While I was in the hospital I did a fourth step, which is an inventory of my current character defects as well as an acknowledgement of the new behavior that I've learned. I began to realize that I'd experienced a lot of hurts even before I turned 20 and thought about doing a life review with my therapist, going back over all the situations where I'd let myself be used and abused. I remembered the occupational therapist saying, "When we do not take care of ourselves, we become dependent on someone or something else to take care of us, and in that we give up control and power." I had done this over and over and still, however subtly, I have been codependent. I have allowed myself to be shamed for who I am, because I believed someone else's definition of me, rather than my own. I have given myself up, over and over and over, hoping in some promise of good, that would never really materialize.

I was in the process of deciding what I wanted to do in my current intimate relationship. It had been hurtful for me not to feel close most of the time and to have to acknowledge to myself that it was very much my effort that held us together. She would refuse to be accountable and avoid taking responsibility for her behavior. It seemed that she was often on the defensive, making me "the loser" so she could "win". I did not want to struggle with her for a position of "power over." This was not my idea of a loving coupleship. I did not want to continue putting my energy into this. I needed to develop boundaries with her that I hadn't had before. Dr. Schuster was telling me that I had my priorities mixed up; "1st. comes self care, 2nd. The relationship and 3rd. the other," he said. I need to put myself first now. I need to use my energy to take good care of me.

Journal entry-Monday, March 13th, 2000

It's Monday night late, really Tuesday morning, 1:30ish am. and I am home!

It all started at about 2:30pm. today with my session with Mark and Dr. Schuster. Both of these men have really been there for me 100% and I am most grateful. Another example of my Power Greater working in my life.

I said good-bye to Mark, who was the interviewing person and my first contact with professional staff down in the intake room last Wednesday (coincidence'? hardly!) He reminded me that it is because of all my hard work and learning in my recovery program that I was able to bounce back from this relapse / recycling process so quickly and so well. He echoed what I want to believe so much intellectually, while I fight down this shame, gut level, that just wants to discount my progress and take me way back. He said it is not a setback or a failure of some kind, but rather is a testing of and an affirmation of my strength / my progress in becoming more balanced and healthier, better able to take care of myself than I used to be. Sure feels good to have someone in this kind of setting recognize that.

I took the bus home at about 6:00 O'clock that evening. Only two people from my life had known where I had been and neither of them knew where I was going. I wanted it that way; wanted to reclaim some sense of my privacy and dignity and freedom. I no longer wanted to kill myself or thought that I should. I just wanted to be home and to be peacefully alone.

By three weeks out of the hospital, I had told only a very few people. I still felt some shame, even though my mind overrides that with the message that I did a good thing to know I was in trouble and needed help. I faithfully took the new medication and felt well, a simple sense of "evenness." I even thought this might have been part of the reason I needed to go back in; that I'd probably built a tolerance to the antidepressant I'd been taking for six years.

Dr. Schuster had said he didn't consider my being there to be any question of morality at all, but rather a case of chemical imbalance that something could be done about.

What a relief to hear that kind of thinking as an inpatient. In the second week at home, I realized I was having an adverse reaction to the new drug. I called the pharmacist and checked symptoms. I was right. I was pissed. I had hoped that this could continue to help.

I made an appointment with my psychiatrist, Dr. R. Hallston. I had only seen him once before and I do not do my therapy with him, so it was hard to walk into his office after this ordeal. He and my psychotherapist, who consults with him, had both received my discharge report including I'm sure, the information that I had refused to enter into a "no suicide" contract while hospitalized. I was embarrassed.

I began the scheduled decrease of my original antidepressant and educated myself about the new one I would begin in seven days. Meanwhile, I saw my general practitioner and started an antibiotic for the infection I'd picked up. I had a horrible reaction to that medication and it didn't help a bit. I started a new antibiotic.

I had called Charlie and said how much I missed her. She had come over to "visit the sick," bearing gifts of chicken noodle soup, a bunch of fresh spring flowers and two pieces of our favorite bakery. A few days later I was on the phone, saying, "Sweetie, would you give this another try with me? Can we be together again?" The words just popped out of my heart, uncensored. She said, "Yes."

We were back to see Jeffrey the next day. He wasn't surprised, though I'm not sure he was approving. Now I am thinking that I made a mistake. This past weekend was going to be our reunion at her house and absolutely everything about our plans went wrong. Once more I heard her reasoning that covered over the fact that she is entrenched in a "power over" position with me. I don't think that she even has a clue as to her own abusive behavior. But I do know what's going on in me because of it. Finally, I know.

I am not willing to take any more chances with my mental, emotional, spiritual health, because of an involvement with somebody else that does not have my best interest at it's core. However wellintentioned this relationship has been, it is not simply by "the ideals" of either of us that I live. Day to day I have allowed myself to be bounced around, reacting to her or working so hard not to react that I was exhausted. This is not the kind of friendship, even without the romance and sexuality inherent in it, that I want to be in. I have not felt this awful since the days just before I went back into the hospital.

If it has taken all of this to help me re-decide to love and respect myself, then I am humbled by these last few weeks and I am grateful. I have said "no more" to another abusive relationship and I have gotten myself solidly back to the very basics of my 12 Step recovery program, reinvested and already recognizing the promises coming true. There is a Guiding Power moving through my life that is Greater than I know. I took a walk in the sunshine today. I sat in my favorite church, empty this afternoon, praying. I was asking for help. I am receiving it right now. Blessed Be...

Part II

Journal entry-Sunday, April 30th, 2000

What the hell am I doing here? It's 10:00pm. What was it that threw me over the edge? This unrelenting pain / my feeling of loneliness made so much worse by being uncared about by my "quasi girl friend"—as I called her on the phone this afternoon / the spiraling down, down, down into shame. I could feel myself sliding down so fast this afternoon; shame for everything, shame for just being and how much I wanted it all to simply be over.

This up and down and up and down mood swing is just wearing me out. It's been weeks now, since I've gotten out of the hospital, that I haven't had a steady dose of an SSRI (selective serotonin reuptake, inhibitor—a class of antidepressant) in my system. All the side effects of trying all these drugs and none of the benefits. I'm exhausted.

I was sitting down in the admitting room before, thinking— -"I must care about myself pretty much, to be going through all of this in order not to be overdosing and just slipping into sleep forever."

What I am doing here—is giving myself a chance, is keeping myself alive! I don't understand it all, but I do know that I want to keep myself alive.

Journal entry-Tuesday, May 2nd, 2000

Head hurting / hurting / hurting since 24 hours ago. Sunday night I curled up in my "nest" on the floor next to the bed. It was in a corner and felt safer than up there. I didn't even feel like I was crying, but kept wiping tears off of my cheeks and away from my eyes.

Yesterday the muscle spasm medication really knocked me out and that was fine. I think it's taking the edge off this fibromyalgia pain—I don't hurt by just touching my thighs or my arms anymore. My knees and ankles still hurt a lot. I've been asking for pain medication for two days or so, just to get through this. Finally a Dr.'s appointment has been set up for me today. Here I am in a hospital setting and since Sunday, when I came in, I've been in high level pain and still haven't gotten any pain medication. I'm going back on my muscle relaxant because they made a mistake and thought it was an active medication when they read what I reported taking. They offered it to me, starting yesterday morning. Thank the powers that be.

It takes everything I have energy wise, to be keeping track of things like an overview of my own medication in order to sort out what's important for them to know, in order to help me, and what is not. I had my first meeting with my psychiatric team yesterday. The new psychiatrist, a woman, is very real. A Jewish woman I think and I like her.

I had such mixed feelings about being there. On one hand, I was grateful for the others to help me with problem solving and keeping track of all the medication changes. I was most grateful to not have access to any of my stockpiled medication. I felt miserable enough that I might overdose— lay down on my bed to go to sleep and just never wake up. I didn't trust myself. Yet I hated being there on the other hand, dependent on the staff and with all the other patients who were psychotic and loud. There were only two other women who were depressed and I'd say severely. One walked around but didn't speak and the other just sat and stared into space. I felt so "well" by comparison.

This was a sad price to pay in my need to be taken care of and I think that this is what really brought me back there. I wanted someone to "pay attention to me". I wanted to be "found" as I lay in my corner the first night. I wanted to refuse to get back in bed, to say "no" and to kick and yell.

Actually I wish I could have given myself permission to act out, to let go and simply be all this anger that I have stored up inside. I wanted to do something to get myself inside the isolation room and then kick the walls and yell until the anger was all out of me. But I just couldn't explode. I had too much control going on.

I was able to cry though, in my session with my psychiatrist. There it was, the subject and the tears that I'd pushed down—all about my mother, missing her friendship those days/ her compassion and her true acceptance of me, no matter where I was at. I missed her being alive and well, living in her apartment on Olive. I missed being able to call her and go visit her on Fridays. I missed her interest in and support of me. April was a very hard month that year without her.

Journal entry-Tuesday night, May 2nd, 2000

I looked up awhile ago and there was Terri. What a good surprise. She held hands with me; we hugged and laughed together. She brought me some underwear pants and socks and a shirt of hers to wear. She sat in my room with me for awhile, which sure makes my room a friendlier place.

As she was leaving, I told her about getting myself here and how it was, wanting to take all my pills after Charlie's call saying she wasn't coming. How that scared me so much, I decided to come in. I shared with her what Jeffrey said, "I don't think she is hearing you, after listening to you two talk the other day." And, "All you can do is ask for what you want, clearly." I had been telling him how I'm not getting what I want with her and tried to defend her, justify it, by saying "She doesn't understand where I'm coming from, doesn't get it about me. With Terri today, I was able to go deeper, started to cry, told her "Charlie isn't good for me. So much of what she does or says hurts me, because I've made her so important to me." Told Toni I wanted to be protected for awhile by staying at her (Terri's) house so Charlie couldn't get to me. I don't want to open myself up to her anymore. Terri says that I don't have to be embarrassed about going back to Charlie, that I did and that it's OK.

Journal entry-Wednesday, May 3rd, 2000

Yesterday I had a session with my doctor, Dr. Weisser, and we went over some family of origin history. I told her that three of us, out of six kids, had been in and out of psychiatric institutions. I said that Mom and Dad had both become alcoholics and that I have two sisters who probably are as well and are in denial. What we explored then, was my wondering if I myself were and alcoholic and I told her how, even without being able to answer that question, I had made a decision sixteen years ago to stop drinking.

This morning I went to my first Alcohol and Other Drugs Abuse meeting here on the unit. I had been upset about this and really wanted to talk about it more. I shared about the shame I felt and the guilt, when I really took a look at where I had been with my alcohol use and abuse. The facilitator suggested I attend some AA meetings and talk about my history with alcohol and drugs. He said "We make it so big and important in our minds, but that when we talk about it the energy around it defuses—gets less and less and finally goes away." I know it will help equalize my shame to be with others who have had the same experience in their background, so I'll get a "When and Where" and go to some AA meetings.

Journal entry-Thursday, May 4th, 2000

I'm sitting in my little corner of the big day room, wanting this feeling of cozy safeness and feeling like myself again, to last forever. This is the first time I'm feeling inner strength or capability since I've been here—since at least a week ago. I want to talk with Dr. Weisser more about "being in the womb"—my need to pull in from the outside world / shut out any stimulation / be dark and warm and little. Wanting to be taken care of.

Last night I said yes to Charlie coming to visit. Libby (my daughter) said that it might be good for her to see me here and for me to receive comfort from her. Now I'm not sure I did the right thing. I feel the need to protect myself, guard myself against her. She says she loves me. I don't even know what that means right now. My psychiatrist here says it's okay to say to her, "I need some time right now to sort things out and I don't want to see you until I'm ready." That seems so radical. I don't want to hurt her feelings and I know that is my co-dependency. Dr. Weisser says I need to tell her where I'm at, just like I'm telling her and her student, right then—tell her that I need to take care of me right now.

It was so good to talk with Libby, who is able to deal with this with a certain degree of detachment. She said she feels sad because she can't do anything to help me. She told some of our friends from the group that I'm in the hospital to get help with my medications. She said she played down the aspect of my depression (as I was able to play down my state of crisis to her). In response, I said that and she replied that she knew. We were able to laugh together, both of us sharing my little secret. I'm so relieved that it's out with Libby and that she really does seem okay with it. I told her I didn't want her to come to visit, to see me like this and she agreed, said she herself didn't want to. I was even okay enough to do a little mothering with her about her relationship issues and that felt real good to both of us. Over the phone we sang "I'm the mother and you're the child" and laughed with relief.

I talked with Jeffrey Monday morning. Had left a message for him on Sunday night from the intake room asking him to call me, even though I knew that I wouldn't have privacy to really talk. This connection with him is so important to me that I couldn't even write about it till now. He did call and, oh did it ever feel good to hear his voice and receive his caring. I've only talked back and forth with him twice on the phone and both times was when I was here last time. On Monday, I was able to have a real good exchange.

Jeffrey suggested that I take my desire to be in a nest and let myself creatively visualize it, so I did. My nest is round, about the size of a double bed and has 'soft to the touch' green, purple and pink pillows in it. I can climb in and mush them around to be comfortable, then pull the green blanket up over and all around me and tuck myself in.

Jeffrey says "Yes", that he will be there for me, that he stands ready to support me in whatever way I need. Tells me "No, you are not too much trouble at all. No, I am not going to stop seeing you," and he wonders where I got that idea. He asks if Charlie said more about wanting to set up another date for joint therapy. I tell him I get the feeling that she's putting her energy into avoiding / denial and in not dealing with her issues; that I didn't know if we'd ever be back to see him together. What Jeffrey said is that after listening to how

Charlie and I talk to each other, he too doubts that she hears me. I told him I felt really abandoned by her three times of not being available to / for me last week. He said all I can do is my part, ask clearly for what I want, then I'll know.

Jeffrey's reassurance that he is there for me and his questioning how Charlie's is about coming back in and his support to me, is so important to me. He suggested that I stay as connected as I can to the natural world outside (I'd told him about the corner windows where I can see into the court yard), the birds, sky, clouds, the bursting forth trees, the rich green grass, the yellow dandelions. He said that to stay connected to my body by noticing body sensations, as I remind myself that this is a container for me, keeps me in the here and now. I tell him how I'm practicing breathing.

Very respectfully, he asks how I want to handle phone contact. Would I like him to call me or do I want to initiate contact? I am so pleased that he is making himself available. I told him that I don't want him to call me, that I need to hide for awhile. I did ask him to schedule me in for next Wednesday though, so I'd know I have that time with him, to which he replied "3:00 PM Wednesday is your spot Elizabeth." and that felt so reassuring. He said he'd call Dr. Hallston and let him know I was here, then we hung up.

When Charlie came to visit that night, she brought along a plastic bag with a letter in it from my sister, an Utne magazine and some Nips. She didn't give me anything from herself; no support, no encouragement, no warm hug or holding hands, no "I'm sad for you." She explained that she'd had a hard time getting there, was distracted by an upset stomach and we spent the entire time outside the visitors' bathroom door.

Dr. Weisser had said earlier in the day that it sounded like I felt trapped by my own decision to let Charlie visit me, that I wasn't doing what I wanted to do and that I had a right to change my mind. I didn't. I wanted to see what being with her again would be like in this safe environment. When the time came, I wasn't open at all and kept control with a lot of talking. I didn't want her close to me, not after all the let downs of the last several weeks. Besides, I'd never shared this part of my life with anybody but my therapists and I wasn't about to do it now. Yet, I wished for some magical breakthrough. It didn't happen. I asked her to leave and she was most agreeable.

Journal entry-Friday, May 5th, 2000

Beautiful Terri popped in kinda late last night, bringing me sweat pants so I could wash my jeans and a T-shirt in all the nice dark colors that I feel safe in. Immediately, we reach for each other's hands and laugh with happiness to be together again. I told Terri how I was disappointed in the visit with Charlie, said it seems like she can't give anything from herself and Terri said she's seen and felt that often with her too! Terri's guess is that if Charlie were to be open, in order to give from within to me, she would also be open to herself and she doesn't want to be because of the pain inside. Yup! Charlie and I had a visit where both of us were inside our walls. Yet I did end up hurting anyway, so my walls didn't really help.

I had a session with Dr. Weisser that morning. Leaning forward, arms on the table, I like her a lot. She's very down to earth; dirty tennis shoes, rumpled hair and all. She makes this so much easier. I trust her insight and her wisdom and her directness with me.

Again, I heard from her what Jeffrey has said to me a thousand times, "Maybe Charlie doesn't act the way I think she should act out her love for me, but that doesn't mean she doesn't love me. She just has a different way of showing it. It's not that black and white in real life." She says that I need to express myself to Charlie more honestly, that protecting her is not being honest with her.

Journal entry-Friday, May 5th, 2000

I was able to go out for my first walk today. It was a group OT activity. Oh, it felt good; hot sun on my arms, on my head, the smell of fresh cut grass, sounds of a plane overhead. The gentle hills with their sprinkling of bright yellow dandelions—all of it so wonderful to me. We all stopped for awhile to just enjoy and I lay on my back on the ground, my spine nestled against the earth. I felt truly held by the mothering quality of the earth—very soothing for me.

The last time I was outside was the day I came in, Sunday. It's been 5 days of separation from the natural world and I've missed it so much. I made a wish on a white, fluffy dandelion head and blew it lightly through the air. I brought in three dandelions and have them in a plastic glass on my dresser, along with my Kleenex box, my glasses that are sitting there right now and the twin ducks named November 10th and November 30th. Bright yellow and bright white light. It's cozy. For right now, it's home.

Journal entry-Saturday, May 6th, 2000

It's Saturday. I just asked how to use my "off ward" privileges. I feel almost giddy inside; to be able to sit here, all alone, on this wooden bench in this small courtyard. I smell the blossoms of this flowering tree I'm sitting under, *feel the wind as it blows across my face and billows my hair. I watch shadow patterns of branches, moving across this yellow paper on my lap. Small white petals have fallen and one lands on my hand, another on the page, I rub one between my thumb and forefinger—so smooth / so soft.*

The night after writing that journal entry on a Saturday afternoon, all hell broke loose on 43C. About five of the loudest patients were reved up and going around in circles at top speed. The Puerto Rican man was making his ugly face and spewing out anger at me in Spanish. The tall black woman with her booming voice was telling all the others what to do. The Jesus woman was singing her 1/2 song and 1/2 sentence mantra "Do you hear me now? Listen to me!" Her roommate, on too much medication, was throwing up and falling asleep. My roommate laughed too much and talked too loud, no not talked, she yelled and it was non-stop. Every room I went into trying to find a quiet corner, had a TV blasting and too bright lights in it. Clustering around the nurse's station, sort of swarming it seemed, were all these restless captives. I felt the heavy tension in the air, almost like we were all going to explode, all at once.

Sunday, the tall black woman who's either ignored or been extremely hostile to me, finds me in the sitting room. She plops down next to me and is chatty. We talk about "the evil eye" and our mothers that have died and how the night before she got drunk with a couple others on the ward and they all put on make-up. (AHH—it was more than the pull of the moon!)

Journal entry-Sunday, May 6th, 2000

10:30 AM. on Sunday. No cup of hot coffee. No Sunday morning paper. I hear the Puerto Rican man singing in the isolation room next door.

Journal entry-Monday, May 8th, 2000

Today I'm getting ready to go home. It seemed I went from, "I'm afraid your going to push me out too soon" (wow! That really sounds like a birthing process) to, "I'll be ready to leave on Monday". Since then, I've been ready to go, over ready, separating from this place.

It is raining and dark and windy. The room I'm in is warm. I'm trying to remember how I was when I came in—it seems so, so long ago, way more than seven days.

This recycling thing is really happening for me. I feel like I'm being born again—leaving this womb-like place with Terri today, being taken to her home for a few days and then soon after taking myself to my home where I begin again, one day at a time, to take good care of me. I can help myself do that by this continuing to turn my will and my life over to the loving care of my Power Greater. I am growing in being able to have mercy for myself, in honesty and in humility. I am healing.

I want to define what the crisis was about that brought me in here both these times. If I learn all I can about the stress that seems to precipitate this, I have a better chance of doing something to help myself before it comes to the point of needing to be hospitalized. This has been about; extreme pain, the arthritis and fibromyalgia flares / the big disappointments with Charlie, potential loss of the relationship / the loss of SSRI's in my system when I cut down on medication, the chemical imbalance / the anniversary of my mom's birth, feeling more the loss of her in my living / the assault on the street, the gun and the further trauma of the lineup, loss of my personal safety and last the lack of proper nutrition and quality sleep. Whew!!! That's a lot when I put it all together like this.

What is helping right now and can continue to help me? I'm feeling sad and lonely. I think I am grieving, as there are so many losses. I need to give myself permission to function at a low level right now and to nurture myself with lots of simply being and breathing.

I want to remind myself that it is okay to be and okay to be feeling my feelings. I need to start a daily exercise plan and to regulate my eating (more) and sleeping (less). I need to begin a habit of daily prayer and meditation. I need to continue reaching out to women who understand depression.

I know that the stress, the pain and the depression form a cycle that drains me of all my energy to use what resources I do have. By intervention at any one of these three points, I can break the pattern and this will bring me relief at the other two points too. It is so simple and seems so complicated to remember this formula and to put it into action.

I want to learn to set boundaries more clearly. This means trusting myself and allowing my inner knowing to guide me. I need to affirm my right to say "no" to others and affirm my right to say "yes" to me. I want to act for myself, stick up for myself and protect myself in much more effective ways than I've been able to do before. I know that I can.

Journal entry-Sunday, May 14th, 2000— Mother's Day.

Going back in was hard, so many reminders of times before, but I hadn't anticipated that coming out would also be difficult for me. Tomorrow it will be one week since the day I left the hospital. So much has been happening and at such a fast pace, that I find myself wanting to just "hide out" today, shut myself off from any new stimulation and give myself space to assimilate some of the old.

Around 1:00 PM. Joey called from Ohio. I'd just sat down in my easy chair with the Sunday paper on my lap, to devour. My own comfortable chair again; smooth feel of brown checkered fabric over the rounded arms, head support nestling into the crook of my neck, legs up at the pull of the handle, easy and easing me "home," I don't have to go anywhere today, what a relief. But what will I say about where I've been when my children call?

Which truths will I tell and which will I withhold? Why will I do that? Is it to protect them from another round of feelings about my mental illness or is it to protect myself from their response, what ever it might be? I do not like my children to know this about me, yet I wrote the letter telling them because I really do believe it is their right to know me as I am. It's just hard. I want to be so capable and independent in their eyes. I don't want them to "worry" about me, to feel a sense of responsibility for "taking care of me" in any way. I don't want them to reject me. I think that this is really what I guard against.

Joe says, a long way into the conversation, "We got your letter." It's my cue and I'm able to say that I didn't want Libby to have to be the only one to know. Joe agrees, it's better *if she can talk about it with them. I bluntly refer to the psychiatric hospital as "The Asylum." It's my way to take the horribleness of it all that lives inside of me again, after these last two times in, and put it "out there" in a shocking kind of a way that I can make fun of. It invites comment in kind. It's the only way I know how to talk about it with my children and it works. Joe tells me a joke about "nuts." We laugh. I could cry—but I don't.*

Libby calls to say "Happy Mother's Day" even though we shared time and gifts and a card, last night. She is easily diverted, tells me a beautiful story of healing in her relationship. I am so grateful that she's feeling loved these days, able to really enjoy it. Ginny will call I know. It's Mothers' Day for her too today. I hope Amelia makes a big deal of it somehow; Ginny deserves that. Maybe I'll call her. I will be glad when this focus for this day is over. I'm uncomfortable with the attention put onto me. It's especially hard because of the need to acknowledge where I was only a week ago. I still feel shaky; I'm still in the process of coming out.

Just getting into Terri's car last week and driving from the West Side of the city, here to the East Side within 15 minutes, astounded me. All the neighborhoods we past, the storefronts I saw, billboards and stop lights and rows of cars everywhere. So much distance covered so quickly. All the decisions the driver has to make. Too much to take in or have to screen out. This, after a week of living on a locked unit in the hospital is an un-comfortable overload that I know I too, will get used to again, too quickly.

Dinner with Terri that first night at her house—it was my job to set the table while she cooked. We used colorful place mats, real silverware, lit a candle and prayed together.

The taste of the tofu sautéed with just a little miso, fresh green beans, red onions, so satisfying and so pretty to look at. Conversation and normal silences not like in the hospital with the long void with others who have nothing to say. Not the plastic forks and knives. Not the serving of fish offered again, to the "vegetarian." Something else here that I wasn't used to: laughter.

The next morning, standing in Terri's kitchen, I realized with a start that I was holding a coffee mug in my hand. It was gray and blue, very plump toward the bottom and the handle was just the right size to slide all four fingers into and around. The coffee was hot and strong and tasted good. The warm mug in my hand felt comforting. It was the first time in over a week that I held a coffee mug in my hand. Something so simple now was something to treasure.

Another thing I noticed was how the trees had changed in just one week. When I went in, the tiny buds were just beginning to open. Mostly, the branches looked stark still against the sky. I watched one special tree through the big corner window while in the hospital. Literally day by day, the soft green leaves pushed outward and grew bigger. I felt connected to that miracle of life. But I was not prepared for what I saw later, lining West Side streets; trees in full, green grandeur, their roundness defined and flowering white / pink / purple branches already dropping petals on the green grass beneath them. I felt sad, as if a stranger here back in the world again. I had missed this burst of life, this sudden breath of spring.

Being home now these last three days, I have mixed feelings. Everything is mine and in its place. My little one room home is warm and cozy. But I feel lonely and it takes me by surprise. I had been living in community, however crazy it was. Still I was one of many. Then with Terri in her home, so comfortable and full with healing. Then with Charlie, where there was easy touch, companionship, familiarity. Now I'm alone and everything is up to me. I'm not sure that I like it this way anymore.

The quiet here is unfamiliar. I used to crave it, guard it from intrusion. These days it hangs heavy around me. There was so much noise in there; always many voices talking and some singing, yelling at, calling for, announcing / the beep, beep of the food carts in the hall / the blasting of three TVs.— even in my room, my roommate's incessant story telling. Here the quiet feels empty. I feel empty in the quiet here.

Every day there, someone not only was noticing me but also was going out of their way to give me their attention. I had a session with my psychiatrist at least once a day and sometimes twice. She was smart, quick, down to earth and could relate to me immediately. In addition, her student sometimes met with me. I had a physician's exam, blood was drawn and pain medication was prescribed for me. There was a nursing staff assigned to me on all three shifts, often the same one for several days, so we developed rapport. He or she answered my questions, brought me my medications, and heard my complaints. Assistants called me repeatedly, without anger, to get up in the morning for breakfast. I felt nurtured by their effort, for me.

I went to AODA meetings (Alcohol and Other Drugs of Abuse) on my unit and the counselor asked about my addictions and listened to me. He gave me a tool to take home and develop that's most helpful. The OT (Occupational Therapy) person invited me to go for an outside walk with her and put her hand on my arm to guide me away from a truck backing up in a driveway. During my first 72 hours in, I was on suicide watch. Every 15 minutes one of the NA's (Nursing Assistant) checking on me to make sure I was there and alive. I knew there that I counted that I mattered that it made a difference if I were alive or dead. They took my pills away; they took my shoelaces and the strap on my bag and my long scarf away. I felt safe there.

Yes, it was an artificial environment. But I got something there that I very much needed and it helped me at the time and enabled me to know I was ready to leave it behind. What was it exactly? Attention? The affirmation that I was important to someone, even though it was there? A response to my being in the world? Is this the sense of loss or loneliness I feel? I am sad that I needed these things so much, that I had to put myself into a psychiatric hospital to get them. How do I give this to myself now? How do I create my life so that these needs are met? This is my challenge today.

Part III

I wondered how many times I would need to go back into the hospital, wondered if I would have to keep going through this over and over for the rest of my life. I didn't want to keep on living if this was going to be my life. I knew that I had the choice about continuing to live or dying, right in my hand

I was asking the deeper questions now: What needs to happen so that I can keep myself out of the hospital? How do I go about creating the quality of life that I want in order to feel at peace with myself? What can I do to allow myself to experience the freedom I long for in order to pursue fulfilling my creative destiny? In the mix, it was paramount that I learned to live in the space in-between having direction and giving up my desire to have control. It was a journey of the soul in transformation, this life. I was leaning toward renewal.

It had been three and a half weeks since I came out of this last hospitalization and it had been hell. The deep, deep depression worse by far than what I'd been going through before I checked myself in. Then I was angry and I had some fight left in me. After that first week or two being out, I barely stumbled through each day. It was a major challenge just to do what was in front of me; get out of bed in the morning (having to lift my heavy body out of the warm and safe and comforting cover of sleep) / drink coffee and hope that the second cup could equalize the downward pull of the medication (increased while in the hospital, added to and then taken away from) and look in my calendar and at my lists to remember what work I had assigned myself for each day.

I did not want to live like this, with this degree of despondency. I had tried to explain to a friend that when one is suicidal, one is already cut off from the energy of others, by their self-imposed isolation. Life cannot continue to flow to anyone who refuses to believe in its transformative power. Hope lies in connection. With others in a circle, holding hands, we can trust letting go of ourselves just enough to allow for some movement and change—like a breath of fresh air. Without change, patterns from the past repeat over and over, slowly and surely an agony without end. Then in self-recrimination, judgement and shame, there is nothing left but to continue the spiraling downward process of dying.

I had told Jeffrey that I was feeling slow change within me. I sensed a landscape ahead. All open in an expanse of possibility. I had realized for the first time in my life, that I could have everything I wanted. I was very afraid to let myself move forward into this belief. He said, "Of course you are, you've had very little experience with feeling ease in your life, with having the sense of fulfillment you're talking about." He goes on to say again how we live in familiar patterns. No blame. He teaches me to think in a new way and to even say out loud,

"I notice that I am feeling afraid to move into the unknown. I seem to be keeping myself in the behavior I know and the familiar feelings that go along with it. This is what is happening right now." It sounds almost like a prayer of forgiveness to myself, like a meditative chant of acceptance. Jeffrey is teaching me to simply be and to love myself exactly where I am in my process. Wow! This is melting the edges of my well-worn perceptions. Over the previous few days I had felt myself beginning to surrender to something deeper, something more true. There was a spark of light nearby that was affirming me.

The day before that I followed through on my commitment in therapy, to tell my group in outpatient treatment that I had been isolating and that I was suicidal. It was really hard to ask for time and then to force myself to talk about the behavior I wanted to hide because I was feeling such shame about it. There was respectful silence. Later on in art therapy, I talked about my ability to give the impression that everything in okay with me when it's not. We were talking about perception. I said how self-defeating my camaflouge was because it kept me from getting the real help that I needed. Then I cried and told more about refusing to let anyone in and wanting just to be dead. The psychiatric OT(occupational therapist) furrowed up her brow and made wonderfully sympathetic sounds. That meant a lot to me. She had heard me.

Jake, another outpatient, had heard me too. He found me standing in the hall, glasses in my hand and feeling like I was in a daze. I knew I was supposed to be somewhere but I didn't know where. When he asked me if I was okay, I told him the truth, "No, I'm not." "I think you need to talk to somebody," he said and stopped the group facilitator as she came down the hall. She took me to the desk and found somebody for me to talk to. Oh my god, people were noticing me and helping me. This was scary. I wait for Joan in the sitting room, the one with the daisies I saw that first night I was here. What the hell was I going to say? "I don't want to live anymore!" No, that sounds too dramatic. "I know this isn't good for me. But I've been really isolating myself and now that I'm here around people who care about me, I'm afraid to go home and be all alone again." No, that sounds too childish. I have another long, loud wailing cry and pull out the blue overstuffed chair and curl up on the floor in the corner. I wanted to stay in that corner forever and ever. My stomach hurt and I wanted my mother.

The day before that I had asked my intimate other to go to my therapy session with me. I had realized after being discharged form the hospital last time, that the staff there had never offered us the same kind of "family session" I'd seen other couples having. Because we are non-traditional, maybe they never thought of us in those terms. Anyway, I wanted to include the person I love and share my life with, in the process of my recovery. I had always wanted to shut her, everyone, out before this. Now I was learning how to let people help me. It was very hard for me to do.

It was there that I told Jeffrey I was keeping myself alive because my daughter Libby had told me that if I killed myself, she would kill herself, too. She and I were together at my house the night before when she said it. I put my hands on her shoulders and looked into her eyes to see if she was telling the truth or just saying that to give me a reason to live and I asked her about that. "I really would Mom, if you die I don't want to keep on living. I need you too much right now." Jeffrey asked if she had any children, shook his head and said to my partner; "Statistics are high for second generation suicide." I feel really scared now with the weight of this added responsibility.

Jeffrey told me that I could call him for an extra session on Friday or the following Monday if I wanted to. He helped me plan how I was going to spend my next couple of hours, how I was going to get through the night. He asked me to tell my therapy group the next day, what I was dealing with. He reminded me that I was a strong woman and that I had gotten through much worse than this before. He looked deeply into my eyes and I felt the impact of his message to me, that I can go through this and that I can survive. His belief in me helped me tremendously.

The day before that I turned off my alarm clock on a Tuesday morning and slept until 1:00 in the afternoon. It was the third Tuesday in a row that I had missed my therapy group in the outpatient program. This time I didn't even call them, I was too ashamed. It was then that I called Jeffrey to ask for the Wednesday appointment. I knew I was in trouble. For five days I'd been refusing to even listen to my incoming phone calls. I just wasn't able to deal with anything more.

The night before that Libby and I had talked on the phone. She said, "Mom, you aren't going to leave me too, are you?" Here is my precious daughter, recoiling from rejection by her seriously indulgent man friend / lover who now wants to be alone. She above all had a right to totally fold up in my arms and expect me to be able to take care of her. I answered quickly, "No Libby, I am not going to leave you. I had been thinking about suicide again and you must have somehow known. But I hear you now and I am making a new decision. I will stay here and you can count on me to walk with you through this and to hold your hand." We both cried a whole lot. There had been a freedom in connecting like this over the telephone.

As soon as Libby and I hung up I called my best friend Terri. Sobbing, I try to apologize for not having been available to her lately and said, "I just promised Libby that I wouldn't kill myself and I can't stay alive without you!" We began again to talk or leave messages almost every day after that. I felt her tender love and respectful acceptance of me, just as I was. Her loving helped me remember how to love myself.

I'd been exhausted. I felt like I was having a huge relapse. I was very seriously depressed. I just wanted to give in and give up. Everything was hard. Getting up out of my chair and walking across the room was almost more than I could do. But I pushed myself forward either out of commitment to other people or out of knowing that if I didn't, that would be the end. All I wanted to do was sleep and be unconscious. I'd wake up and my first thought would be "Oh god, another day I wish that it was over and I'd be going back to sleep." I'd been taking trazadone at night. I could feel it's sedating effect washing over me. I knew I didn't need it anymore to sleep. I counted out the pills to see how long it would last me.

Easter weekend was horrible. I wanted to be dead. I worked at my retail sales job all day on a very busy Saturday. By surprise, my boss worked that day too and he noticed everything. I made stupid mistakes at the register, entering my sales number incorrectly over and over. Each time the error buzzer rang he came from his office to fix it. I gave incorrect change to impatient customers and then wasn't able to open the cash drawer to compensate for it, while they stood there and waited. On Sunday, I dragged myself through a traditional "family" dinner with my sweetheart, her mother and my daughter. It was pure agony. I had almost nothing to add socially and responding took everything out of me. The very last thing in the world that I cared about was that it was a holiday of transformation and rebirth. The tag on my new silk blouse scratched the back of my neck all afternoon and to top it all off, even the ham wasn't redeeming.

I wondered where I had gone wrong. Had that wonderful high that I left the hospital on, evaporated into this air? I had been out now, up until Easter. What had been happening to bring me crashing down like this? I knew I had been too busy, even though I'd had the best intentions to pace myself. I went back to work and then went ahead and facilitated the workshop that I had planned the month before. I spent a chunk of time with my intimate other, then with my sister. I wrote lists and tried to make some new kind of schedule for myself. I finally got the dishes done that had been sitting on my sink since before I went into the hospital. Then I got sick. My body gave out and gave in to the flu that lasted for days. I talked with my other daughter in Ohio, on the phone. My brother called me from Washington. I went back to my CoDA meeting. I got a letter from my landlord saying I owed a late fee for having paid my rent in two installments the month before. I got a letter from my psychiatrist saying I owed a fine for having cancelled my appointment the week before. It was too much. I just wanted to stop. Being dead seemed the best way to do that.

Part IV

It was so much easier being an "in-patient" on 6 West, the psychiatric floor of Columbia/St. Mary's hospital. It was more than coincidence of course, to have checked my self "in" there. The original St. Mary's Hill psychiatric hospital where I'd had my first admission more than 30 years ago, had moved to the East Side a while back and now merged with services at the other fine, old hospital on Milwaukee's East Side, Columbia. Within my family as well as within our community, there was a general feeling of trust and pride in the long-standing fine reputation of both hospitals.

That morning before my appointment with Jeffrey, I'd called the business office there to see if they would accept my insurance. In spite of the fact that I was limited by having only the "poor peoples" insurance, I knew that I could absolutely not go back out to the County Mental Health facility, where I had been very much warehoused twice last year. I asked if my Title IX insurance would cover me being admitted on an emergency basis and found out it would.

In spite of the fact that Jeffrey tried to steer me towards going to the home of my friend Terri, who had offered to take me in and take care of me should I have the need for safety and nurturing again, I went to the hospital. Jeffrey said he suspected that to turn to strangers was easier for me than to ask for and receive help from someone who knew me and would say "yes" to me. He was right. I was so afraid of the dependency needs I have always felt in myself, that to allow that part of me to be known to my best friend in the whole wide world, was more of a risk of rejection than I could possibly handle right then. It was an equal risk of acceptance and love that I was terrified of as well. I could not let anyone get really close to me. To even be able to

The Crazy Quilt

turn to my therapist with all this was the result of years of testing and the building of trust.

So after assessing the state of crisis I was in and asking if I wanted his help in getting myself into a hospital, Jeffrey let me know that he was proud of me for taking on the responsibility of making a good choice for myself and we said good bye. I had permission to call him at any time in my need and we had set up an appointment two days from then. My long, slow walk in the neighborhood of small homes and neat gardens in front of them was thoughtful and deliberate. I stood for awhile next to the gravesite of my old "friend" in the small, 100-year-old cemetery I visit regularly. Did I want to stay alive? I think I heard the "caw-caw" of some of the black crows I so love, my "god" birds, or else I just imagined that I did.

I felt wonderfully free. It seemed like some weight had been taken off of my shoulders. I turned my collar up to fend off the March winds, put my hands in my pockets and walked and walked and walked. On the bus, I still didn't really know what to do but I felt okay about that. I knew whatever I decided to do would be right. Later, I sort of surprised myself when I got off on Hartford Avenue and started my trek to the emergency room entrance of Columbia/St. Mary's Hospital.

Inside the glass doors, down the short blue hallway, at the small 1/2 door window, I felt scared. Said, "I'm here because I'd like to be admitted to the psychiatric unit." (Yikes, I said that so calmly, as if I actualy know what I'm doing!) The nurses were accepting of me right where I was at and efficient. That made it all so much easier, almost "matter-of-fact." I was asked if I was suicidal, sharp things were taken from me, an "in-house" psychiatrist called to make an assessment and while I waited in an examining room, a security officer was stationed outside.

It was a long wait; I wondered if they had forgotten about me. This security guy was an old codger who guarded his lunch bucket at his feet and while he sat on his folding chair next to the open door, seemed totally oblivious to me. I didn't quite know why he was there, it was obvious that he was incompetent if his job was to "guard" me and I felt anxious and angry.

"Okay", I said to myself, "I'm here because I do not have control of my actions, so I might as well act that out." I must admit it was fun to be devious and see what I could "get away with" before this guy noticed. I moved slowly and quietly across the room, slid open a drawer in a small supply table and found what looked like a needle for a syringe, inside a red plastic case. "Ha, I won!" I said to myself, just as he turned his head and told me in a tired voice, "Don't be touching that now," and I answered, "Oh, I'm just looking." I liked having a "weapon" down deep in my blue jean pocket, though I had no idea what I was going to do with it.

The examining doctor finally arrived. I told him the truth about how awful I felt and not really wanting to kill myself, but the pills being at home, my resistance being low and my need for safety being so high right now. To my surprise, my psychiatrist is on staff here. I'd known it was a posability but I really hadn't counted on that being a help to me. They called him and he agreed to admit me. Oh god, I was glad. Somebody heard me; somebody was right there to help me. I no longer had to go through this agonizing trial, so all alone. A short, dark haired, "with—it", friendly woman from security came, to take me up to 6 West.

That first night and first day was easy. I felt safe. I began to relax. Maybe still the relief of being taken seriously; staff people around whom wanted to help me, who felt competent and knew what to do. Then I'm not sure quite what happened inside or when exactly, or how, but I began to feel scared again, desperate, mistrusting and alone. I spent a lot of time in one of the small lounges near the nurses' station. In spite of the open blinds on both windows and the security checks on me every 15 minutes (I'd immediately been put on a suicide watch), I was intent on hurting myself and on doing that without the staff noticing.

That became my primary intent. It wasn't at all choice, but rather a driving force from down deep inside me. I was violently angry, I knew that. I remember my mother saying the word "violent" sometimes when she spoke about anger and I'd always thought it an over dramatization. It wasn't. Yet I could only let that out in small and silent, deviant bursts of relief. It helped some, but not a lot. It's extremely hard for me to talk about this. I began to cut myself with whatever I could find that would break the skin and draw blood. It was the first time I've ever done this and I did it with a determined fury.

Staff became angry with me. I didn't care. I became more inventive, hiding instruments of torture so that I'd have access to them later. I knew there was something "crazy" about my behavior in this kind of setting, some eventual futility, but I needed to do what I was doing. Maybe it gave me some kind of purpose, a reason for being. They were the enemy now and I wanted to win.

I said "no" to everything they offered to do to assist me, to calm me and to curtail me. I liked saying "no". I liked refusing to co-operate. I liked acting so angry. I liked watching them not sure what to do. All of the sudden, they did. Four or five people came rushing at me, pulling on rubber gloves. I was confused. What was going on? I was being grabbed by big bodies, held back in unrelenting grips, my hand pried open, forced to my knees, pulled onto the mattress, held down. I tried to pull away. I had to do something but I didn't know what. I banged my head on the floor over and over. Somebody lifted my head onto the bed.

We struggled twice like that on two different nights. In between, I'd pull the plastic leaves off of the plant, thinking maybe I'd eat them. The top of a plastic fork drawing bright red blood. The angry nurse yelling at me, "This is enough now! Do you feel so afraid that you need to be restrained to feel safe?" The sound of the metal buckles closing. They moved in a bed, threaded the wide red straps into openings. I kept trying to sit up, to fight back. One of the male nurses kept pushing me back down too hard, his hand on my chest. I was so damn pissed. One of the times during being held by the wall, Sheila gave me a shot. I vaguely remember someone sitting outside the door or next to me, while I slept.

I paced. They said I seemed to get anxious right around the time of the shift change late in the afternoon, when a lot of commotion was going on. They offered Zanex and it calmed me. They taught me to notice what was going on inside and to ask for help, medication or a staff person to talk to or to take some "time out." Little did they know that telling what was going on with me and asking someone to care about and then help me, was the most difficult challenge in my world. Maybe they did know. I still wasn't sure if I liked any of them, if I could trust them.

My own admitting doctor listened to me. He was warm, kind and astute. He asked questions about my childhood, my family and took lengthy notes. He answered my questions and explained to me what was happening. His easy manner reassured me and there were even times we could laugh together. I began to relax.

There was a staff meeting, me in my hospital gown and four of them dressed in regular street clothes: "Elizabeth, the goal here is to have you take more of the responsibility for monitoring yourself, knowing you have choices and beginning to use new behavior. We want you to realize that it's okay to ask for help. We're going to push you and you may not like it. Just when you adjust and then get comfortable, we're going to push you again. Later you'll feel better off because of it. You're learning to function better in here and will be able to in the outside world, too." Oh, so this is what "being in treatment" is all about. What the hell have I gotten myself into?

The psychiatrist, who I didn't like, taking over while the unit doctor was on vacation, called me aside to confront me. "Elizabeth, you need to live up to your contract of asking for help when you're feeling like hurting yourself. If you continue to "act out", then maybe this is not the place for you to be." I felt really scared. Asked, "Where would I go? Are you going to just throw me out on the street?" She replied, "To have to use restraints here, is very unusual. We want people to be taking responsibility for monitoring themselves, knowing they have choices and using new behavior." This sounds very familiar.

After my session with her, I walk down the long hallway, sobbing. I don't know how to be different. They want me to talk, to tell them, to trust them and I just can't. Jerry, another patient who has befriended me, comes up and puts his arm around my shoulder, walks me to the nurse's station. Jim is there, stands up and I tell him how scared I am. He gets it and says, "You're scared you're going to get kicked out? No, we're gonna hang in there with you Elizabeth. We're not going to give up on you!" Oh god, I needed so badly to hear that right then and Jim knew. Maybe somebody here does care about me. Jim seems solid, sincere and I'm beginning to trust him.

That last week and a half or so, was so much easier. The crisis past, off the suicide watch, out of the empty, gray concrete seclusion room and into my own room with patterned wallpaper and soft draperies, carpet on the floor, my own private bathroom and a telephone. I could wear my own clothes, wash and dry them, had my shoelaces back. I was allowed to go to groups now, eat my meals with the others, have china plates and real silverware, watch TV if I wanted to and best of all, hang out and visit.

I met good people there that I'll never forget. We helped each other in our healing. In fact, we could not have done it without each other. As good as the staff turned out to be, it was in the camaraderie of others who knew how it was to live with mental illness, that we found comfort and humor and hope.

Jerry introduced himself to me, my first day there. I backed away from his friendliness, thinking, "Oh god, a cling on has found me already." But after my worst days were nearing the end, I was more open and glad for his presence. There weren't many people my age there, I was lonely and I must admit, I enjoyed his attention. What made it safe was that he had a "girlfriend" on the outside and so did I. Even better was that he was going to be traveling through Europe all summer. We made plans to get together, to call each other. He gave me a gift. I was very sad for days after he left. He's sent me a postcard and called, since I've been home. He was filled with kindness. It frightened me. I haven't responded.

There was a small group of women that was very special to me. The four of us "clicked" so easily, bouncing off of each other with our sharp wits and enjoying one anther's story telling. We'd sneak off to the music room at dusk, so nobody else would see us and want to join in. Then we'd line up chairs in front of the big window facing west, and together every night, watch the sun slowly go down. With "Ohhs" and "Ahhhs" and sometimes silence and sometimes ruckus laughter, we shared our evening ritual. As one by one, each of us began to leave, we witnessed the emptiness where she had been with us, so fully.

By the time I left, nothing was the same as it had been. I felt sad about that and at the same time, glad. I'd been "in" for only two and a half weeks and had experienced so much that was to change my life, the linear time line seemed almost artificial. My utter aloneness had melted into appreciation of this complex community that I was an important part of. That was the most difficult aspect to have to say good bye to. A few of us had exchanged phone numbers and hugs, yet it's a different reality "out there" and we were letting go of what had been. Staff people I'd been afraid of and later angry with had become advisaries, sources of encouragement and comfort. I went to some of them or they walked across a therapy group to me and we shook hands.

The three small, gray rooms of the seclusion unit that at one time had meant safety and comfort, later panic and power over, now were just three empty rooms behind their locked doors. I was on the outside, looking in and remembering. The occupational therapy room, so full of color and tactical pleasure and soft voices, had allowed me to explore. Our springtime kites, with flowers and kittens on them, lined the long hallway. The small sitting rooms had plastic upholstry, I'd discovered. The basket of white daisies was still there and as I left, they brought back the plant I'd been pulling the leaves off of. I chuckled. What was I going to do with a pocket full of plastic leaves? I had been so desperate.

Security brought up my money and keys. It was the same short woman with the warm smile. We talked again about her great fountain pen. Our meeting now seemed so long ago. I signed forms. Lonnie asked me to put my hand in his, and he did a little dance with me as only Lonnie could, calling it "the last dance with me." I was charmed. I was free now and it was time to go. I walked through that unit door and went down in the elevator all-alone. Taking my time now, breathing space, feeling myself being free space. It was a beautiful, sunny afternoon and there was my sweetheart, sitting behind the wheel of her car, waiting for me.

My children have come closer to me. I wrote to them shortly after I was out, asking them to write, saying that in my wanting to protect them from more tragedy in my life I had inadvertently shut them out. I got very honest and told them I was aching with loneliness for each one of them and; their families. They've been calling more, stopping by, sending things in the mail. The flow of energy feels good all around, natural, not like a "rescue."

My oldest daughter asks me long distance, "Mom, what caused it?" (The emotional breakdown, this one.) "There must have been something inside that was bothering you."

I had to tell her, "Well the truth is, I really don't know." I had made a list of all the precipitating factors in the letter to my kids, trying to help them understand; lots of stress, being too busy, lack of sleep and good food and any exercise, the absence of sunshine for months, cutting down on medication, worry about money, isolating myself, being tired all the time, loss of hope that anything would ever be any different, wanting to give up the struggle. But I had to tell her the deeper truth, that I really don't know.

It was the most valuable lesson I learned while in the hospital this time. No one really knows what causes mental illness and accounts for the cyclical patterns of it's symptoms in a person's life. The subject of extensive research and multiple theories over time, mental illness still remains somewhat of a mystery and out of grasp in our very human need to have control over it.

Dr. Brown said it so eloquently at the end of group that last day and I paraphrase her here: 'Our symptoms and the types of illness we experience may be slightly different, as we each express ourselves in our own way. Yet we all share similar characteristics that everyone in the population experiences, to some extent. The difference is that for us, the degree that this manifests itself is causing us severe difficulty in our daily lives. The reason for that, nobody really understands. It has to do with genetics, yes, inherited tendencies toward obsessive-compulsive disorders, addictions, depression and suicide, just like being at high risk for diabetes, high blood pressure, heart conditions and cancer. It has to do as well, with growing up in the families we did, ways of responding we learned, habit patterns we've developed and the extent of trauma we've experienced in our lives. One aspect affects the other in terms of brain waves, chemical imbalances, mood disorders and even the circumstances of whether we live or die.

What we do know is that some of us continue to live with mental illness and that it isn't our fault. Yet we each have the responsibility to take care of ourselves to the best of our ability; to learn all we can about how to help ourselves function more effectively and stay well. When we need help with that, it is up to us to reach out and make use of the many forms of education, treatment and hands-on support that is available to us, in the mental health community at large as well as through general medical and alternative health resources.'

This time going in again and then coming back out, I really want to be my last time. But I don't know if it will be, in spite of my renewed vigilance to all areas of my living. The help I was able to receive this time far surpassed any of my other in-patient experiences. I feel better equipped, more prepared to maintain my balance. Yet I don't know what life may have in store for me, just like I haven't understood until more recently, just where I've come from. The life saving grace of this experience is that I have absolved myself of the heavy burden of my shame.

Part V

Journal entry-Sunday night, October 21st, 2001

I am feeling so much better. It's 10:45 or so at night and I'm sitting in my bed listening to air pushing through the vents under the window next to me. Warm air, finally. I like the steady, calming whoosh! I'm waiting for this trazadone to knock me out and it's a pleasant, slow sinking. This has been a tremendously hard day.

I fought with myself all afternoon, pushed myself out of this warm, dark room by the third call to group this morning. God, I didn't want to be in there, with people I don't know, in this hospital gown and with these stupid black socks on, my hair not brushed for I don't know how many days. But I pushed myself to therapy group because I know that I have to—that this is a disease of isolation. I have boldly told my close ones, Terri and Libby, not to come here and not to call. I left a message at the desk that I do not want to receive any calls from Charlie. I knew that at the least, I had to face knowing what other patients are here. It's been so quiet on the floor that it's creepy. So I went to therapy, sat there split off from me and everyone else, said my name and that I knew being here in group was better than being in my room, cutting myself. God, that's a hard thing to say.

This afternoon all I wanted to do was climb inside the dryer or lay my cheeks up close against the warm washing machine and rock and rock back and forth to sooth this thinking that won't stop in my brain. As I'm writing this, it sounds really desperate and wacky, but at the time it seemed the perfectly logical thing to do. I wanted to say to this warm water sloshing, white smoothness, "Are you my mother?" It's a line from a child's book; this lost child is saying to everyone and everything, "Are you my mother?" as she tries so hard to find her safe place in the world. For me, this afternoon, the closest I got was clinging to that wash machine and dryer. They say we know exactly what we need. I did. Womb therapy. I gave it to myself in the small, warm laundry room.

That Sunday had been very hard for me. I felt desperate. Nobody knew I was hiding in the laundry room, running thin pieces of basket weaving material and white plastic forks, up the insides of my arms. I wanted to be stopped from hurting myself. Finally one of the staff found me and called Sheila, my nurse, who suggested the anti-psychotic medication, saying "Let's get some in there and see if it helps".

The nurse that she'd asked to stay with me while she called my doctor irritated me with her matronizing comments and finally I told her to stop talking to me and to stop touching me. All I wanted to do was to keep rocking against the warm wash machine.

Sheila was back, asking me if I'd hurt myself already and asking me to give her what I'd used. When I refused, she called for help and told someone to call security. When I looked up there were four or five staff people, standing very close to me in a circle and I felt scared, cornered and mad. Then some soothing voice said "Come on now Elizabeth, we're taking you to the security room and you can either come along with us calmly and save your dignity or we can force you to come with us and make a big scene and we don't think you want that—so give us what you have in your pocket".

When I would not, some middle aged man in a blue uniform with badges on grabbed my left forearm and this nurse that I hate wrapped her hand around my right wrist and I tried to force open her damn fat fingers. I was forcibly being moved out of the laundry room and down the hall. No matter how hard I resisted, they won't let go.

They left me alone in the security room, but I didn't want to be left all alone. I ran my thumbnail across the mesh screen on the inside of the window. It was loud but it wasn't helping just to be loud so I went to the door to pound on it and found it open a crack. I boldly walked down the hall to my room and suddenly someone was calling that I was in the hall while someone else was locking my bedroom door and Sheila was behind me, saying, "I'll get you a pillow and do you want a blanket? You can lie down here near the nurses station".

I was childlike then, wanted this nurturing nurse like a big sister, to keep taking care of me, keep being kind to me. She said she'd check back with me in half an hour and we'd know then how the medication was affecting me. I lay there feeling comforted, staff people nearby and I heard their voices. I closed my eyes and sunk into the hum. When I woke up, oh I felt so much better that I want to sob and sob with relief at how I felt being "normal" again, with how good I felt to be liking myself, how good it was to be back in my body feeling finally, like me.

Journal entry-Wednesday, October 24th, 2001

I'm getting ready to call Charlie. I know she's not home and I'll get the answering machine, but still I'm feeling scared to be so definitive so I practice in my mind. "I've realized while here that a short separation from you would be good for me, a chance for me to just pay attention to what I need, as different from putting my relationship with you at the forefront of my mind. I'm thinking about two weeks of not seeing each other and not talking on the phone. You can leave messages with my answering machine or we could E-mail. If we want to we could go out of town over my birthday weekend, get to know each other again." Yikes, what if she gets so mad at being pushed aside, that she just wants to break up with me. Oh well, that's the consequence of asking for what I want.

Journal entry-Thursday, October 25th, 2001

Today I'm going home and still a big part of me doesn't want to. Safety issues are not a concern to me now. Yes, I'll have access to my sharp little paring knife at home, where as here even the plastic knives are "verboten" to me, but I don't feel desperate anymore and I have no interest in making anymore scars on the insides of my arms. The other stress that brought me back in here, was being so stuck in my head analyzing and trying to control this relationship that I became obsessed with the problem. Right now, the last thing that I want to do is to put any "work" into this relationship. My interest now is in me, making sure that I use my support network to talk about me, to know I'm worth that time and attention and to ask for it and use it. I want to be soothing and comforting to myself right now, even to play.

What I don't want to give up here, are the comfort of others around and the nurturing of the staff. It is being taken care of that is filling such a need in me, my lost inner child, finally in family with sisters and brothers and parents who care about me, who are helping me take care of myself.

It's these small, simple things that I'm going to have to give up: Brad opening the door of my room at 8:00 am;

the bright hall light following him in, his warm smile and "careful not to be too cheery" attitude helping me start my day. "I brought in your morning medications, Elizabeth," handing me the small plastic; cup with two tablets and one capsule in it, color, shape, a paper cup with water in it—just this feels like love and kindness greeting me at the side of my bed every day. The call over the PA system, "11:00 therapy group will be starting in a few minutes." or "Lunch trays are here," or "Elizabeth, Dr. P.A. Hallston is here (by now I had switched to the female part of the husband and wife team) and she'd like to meet with you in the small lounge." I liked having that structure, those reminders about where I needed to be, when. Being just as I was at a therapy group, in my nightgown, hair uncombed, not wanting to make contact; in the art therapy room feeling glad to be drawing. Closing the door of the music room as I listened to the Heart Math tape and being so glad when I was done being alone, that there were people to go back to. Sitting with others after a meal or in our places a long while after group has ended, just because being together feels good, talking, laughing, complaining, even singing and loving each other with, "You can do it." and "Hang in there, it will get better." Pulling up my covers in bed and leaning to turn off the light, loving the total darkness and quietness. Being alone and yet feeling so safe in knowing that in the hallway the lights are on and that down at the nurses' station staff are doing their job charting, measuring medications, talking on the phone—yet mostly being there. Simply being there for me, in case I need them.

I feel so sad, having to give this all up. Having to hoist my heavy black bag over my shoulder and wrap my black scarf around my neck. Having to button my black shirt/ jacket over my olive green "bum" sweatshirt over my green and black flannel shirt over my short sleeved black t shirt (the one I could wear here when I didn't have to hide the slashes on the insides of my arms). Now I have to say my last good-bye, have someone buzz open the thick locked door and walk forward through the portal, even though I don't want to leave any of this behind.

Part VI

Looking over my journals, I'm aware again that it had been months of building up to this recent crisis. Work in retail over the holidays had been more difficult than the year before. I felt more worn out at the end of a day and my arthritis was flaring up. I thought I felt the effects of midwinter depression setting in and talked with Jeffrey about increasing my time in outpatient groups at the hospital and asking my psychiatrist to up the dose of the anti-depressant I was taking.

My relationship with my partner was not going well. As we celebrated out 10th anniversary of being a couple, I was contemplating having an affair. I never talked about it, other than in therapy. I felt increasingly lonely. By February, I had decided to continue in this relationship and put effort into trying again to ask for and receive the qualities of intimacy that I wanted very much. I knew that this third time would be the last that I would ask her to make a commitment to me and to this relationship. This time her answer was a clear and simple, yes. It was a tremendous relief for me to have crossed that scary edge within myself and I think all of this was just more stress emotionally than I realized at the time.

During January, my dear friend Terri and I were moving closer to making a decision about living together for awhile. She had a big house with porches and a yard and was rambling around in it feeling lonely. I was incredibly sad here with my own loneliness, in a studio apartment that continuing to rent would insure my long standing pattern of financial struggle that I wanted very much to address and change. Terri and I have been close friends for over 30 years. So much about it seemed right.

Yet by the end of February, we both knew that it wasn't going to work. Each of us struggles with severe depression and it became apparent that the danger of bringing each other down in a day to day environment far outweighed the other, healthier aspects of our friendship. We both were able to acknowledge our own growing edges and the value we placed on continuing to learn how to balance our friendship. It was a huge loss for me, even though I knew I was deciding on the best course of action for myself. I realized I'd been in denial about my own unhealthy lack of boundaries and in denial about the severity of my friend's struggle. There would be much grieving to do.

All in all, December, January and February were very dificult months and I found myself in crisis again with my emotional/mental health issues. I'd thought this was over. I'd thought that when I left the hospital this last time, I would never need to be back. I thought I'd learned and practiced my new ways of thinking and behavior enough that I was on solid ground and would stay there. This is the insidiousness of mental illness. My internal struggles and the additional external stressors are never really under my control at all. The best I can do is to keep myself as well balanced as I can on a daily basis and to notice and ask for help as soon in the process as I can when I'm starting to slip. Again I had let small acts of self-care go, without even noticing at the time. Again I had tried to take on more than I could manage at once and I hadn't realized the toll it was taking on me. Again I fell into a deep and despairing depression.

Journal entry-Thursday, January 10th, 2002

Jeffrey reminds me that I'm in a process of 1) wanting to protect and nurture my little spark of light (this new in-balance/ serene/ stable self) and 2) wanting to re-create trauma (old memories of sexual abuse/ currently allowing my boundaries to be violated by giving too much of myself). The old patterns are more familiar—stress, crisis, depletion. Leading to anger with them / with me. Taking it out on myself—self abuse. Leading to going back into the hospital in crisis. Leading to setting up a situation where I can fight against the staff.

Journal entry-Monday, January 14th, 2002

I talk more than I ever have about both cutting myself and my sexual abuse issues in therapy group at the hospital today. I used both groups and was able to get to both topics, the whole lifetime of trauma and crisis that I've lived, how familiar that is for me.

Last night I was doing dishes and ran a knife over my arm, after saying to myself out of the blue, "I wonder how it would be to cut my arm right now." Last Thursday the sexual abuse stuff came up when later, Jeffrey cautioned me not to re-traumatize myself.

Celia asked me so pointedly today, what, besides the familiar did I get out of cutting myself and I had to admit to myself and out loud, that it's the attention I get by being in a victim role and having other people care about me, take care of me. Celia challenges me about what other ways can I get caring from other people—aside from how I'm giving it to myself right now. She points out what a switch it is for me, when I've been in the rescuing and /or caretaking role and says that it might be part of my wanting to be more in balance and needing to figure out how to do that in a healthy way.

Later, Jake pointed out again, how I am unfamiliar with this balanced and serene place I'm in. I recognize the "shadow" side of me because maybe for the first time, I'm not living in it. This recognition is living in the light.

Journal entry-Thursday, January 24th, 2002

I had another good therapy session with Jeffrey today as I'm working this stuff out about living with Terri or not. He teaches me this formula: "What kind of internal experience do I choose to have?" and "What do I do in order to cultivate that?"

I think that I'm going to call him Wilson Zukov because he reminds me so much of both TV's Wilson on Tool Time and Gary Zukov as he nods his head "yes" on the Oprah show. Jeffrey's wisdom and compassion go deep into my heart and soul. I am most grateful to have him in my life.

He goes on to say that the way our memory works is to record sight, sound, smell, taste, touch and that anything similar at any time can trigger remembering and bringing up past trauma. Jeffrey believes that we never heal completely, that the best that can happen is that we are more effectively able to deal with the next incident of trauma, by what we have learned since the initial experience.

He says the best way to survive traumatic flashbacks is to move through the experience being aware and not to re-traumatize myself by going back into the events consciously, but rather to keep my attention here and now. He encourages me to focus on the tools I have at hand to empower myself, to remind myself that I am here right now (not back there, then) and to choose to feel alive, whole and well. I am safe. I am at peace.

Journal entry-Saturday, January 26th, 2002

So many people wanting and needing my attention it just makes me irritable. I'm figuring out that my need / want is to have some control—yes. But not control over any other, rather, in regard to me.

I am protecting myself from having to respond to someone else, having to take care of someone, having to—when I don't feel like giving anything.

In the past in my relationships, I gave myself away. I did not know how to say "no", i.e., symbiotic relationship with my mother, i.e., if I don't take care of her she will die (if my mother dies I won't have anyone to take care of me), therefore my job was to live my life for her. In the past, other peoples' needs have always been much bigger than mine.

Journal entry-Thursday, January 31st, 2002

This morning as I sat with Terri after her testing at the hospital, she told me (again) about her concern for me if I lived with her because of her degree of chronic pain, depression and despair.

I feel so sad for her. Could feel myself begin to go down into depression and that is very dangerous for me. I begin to feel the edge of my own feelings of hopelessness and despair inching closer to my center, my core where I've been experiencing being solid and pride in my personal power and genuine joy.

This is dangerous for me. I feel unable to be truly detached from Terri's thoughts and feelings. I feel scared that if I was to live so involved with Terri's life I might lose myself. This seems like a very important warning to me about what I am trying to decide.

Journal entry-Friday, February 8th, 2002

I'm feeling how angry I am with Charlie for not being ready to live with me, for keeping the door shut on that option for me. That is really what I would like to be doing. I'm realizing that I give up so much power in this relationship that it seems like my intimate other is in charge of my decisions. The truth is in fact, that I am the one who shut the door because I do not feel ready. I forget this, and blame Charlie for not being the person I want, i.e., someone who wants me. I am so afraid to be really close that I'm on the verge of panic. I'm the one who keeps Charlie away from me. I feel afraid of loosing myself and being controlled.

Journal entry-Thursday, February 21st, 2002

There have been a lot of disappointments in my life lately. Sally moving out of town is really a loss for me. I don't think that I've let myself really feel about that yet, She's the only person left in my family that I feel close to. Her leaving puts me in touch with missing Mom.

Pam not wanting to do the Shamonic Journey group with me in women's space, is a big disappointment. First I felt angry with her, then on the defensive to what seemed like her attack on me as a group facilitator, a separatist and another strong woman from a spiritual tradition she doesn't know about.

Then there was Charlie's complete inability to be sensitive and to support me Sunday night when I got off the phone with both Terri and Jeffrey as I simply asked for a hug. It reminded me of the night before, when I sat in the kitchen all *by myself, crying and then sat in the bathroom crying with the door closed and the water running to shut out the sound of the damn computer game.*

All this reminded me how I used to be crying my heart out about some sadness and Joe Sr. would be watching some science fiction thing on TV, totally in his own little protective world, oblivious to me. No wonder after four years of that, I wanted to kill myself.

This, plus the trauma I'm going through about my relationship with Terri right now that is very hard on me. I wrote her a note two days ago, saying I needed some space and time to listen to my own counsel and decide how I wanted to respond to this crisis. I feel a little guilty about pulling away like this, but know that I need to, I'm quite sure I've decided not to live with her, but I'm having a hard time actually owning my decision.

I'm sitting in the hall right now, at the top of the stairway outside of Jeffrey's office while I wait for him to arrive. I'm scared. What else will I find out about myself? Am I ready to know any more? This is all sort of "coming at me" so fast. I want to remember that I am orchestrating this and that I can slow it down for awhile.

I finally did put in a call to my psychiatrist and when she didn't return the call after a couple of hours, I left a message for her husband, my other psychiatrist. I spent most of the afternoon hiding in my little writing room with both doors closed so I could feel safe. I started to pack a small bag to take to the hospital with me. I was very concerned that my urgency to cut myself seemed unstoppable. Dr. R. Hallston returned my call and was patient with me. He was asking a lot of questions, especially as to what had been the trigger to this kind of response. I guessed that it was my contact with Terri in the troubled state that she was in, my concern about her safety and my inability to be of any real assistance to her. He said he'd call me back in half an hour, that he wanted to give Jeffrey a call and have his input into this.

When he called back, I had just made three fresh cuts to my arm and knew I had to tell him about it. I think I was going through some kind of panic where I needed to take action to relieve the tension. I asked him to admit me, if only for the weekend, and he said, "No" so strongly that it frightened me. He said he and his wife had talked and decided that it was best for me to stay out of the hospital and to use the strong support system they knew I had. When I told him I was afraid of cutting myself again, he said, "Well just don't cut too deep," and I was hurt by his seemingly non-caring attitude. He said he'd call back in the morning to see how I was doing and I hung up confused and feeling like I had just been hit in the stomach.

By the next morning I was too angry to pick up any of his three calls, but I did call his answering service to say I was okay and would be at my staff meeting with Dr. P.A. Hallston on Monday morning. It was one hell of a weekend of hiding and feeling hurt even more by what was happening outside of me on top of the turmoil that I felt on the inside. The agony that I went through I can't even put into words. Mostly it was the terrible feeling of being utterly alone in my pain. But I took the increased dose of the anti-psychotic, I did not cut myself again and I did show up for my staffing appointment.

Journal entry-Saturday, February 23rd, 2002

Dr. R. Hallston—I hate you! He calls back and leaves his message so matter of fact that it feels mean to me. I hear again, his voice in my mind, "That's not what the hospital is for. Just don't cut too deep." I think he is suspicious of me, not going to give me what I want, thinks what I want isn't good for me. This feels parental. The strong and emotionally removed father with the desperate and acting out child. I just want to kick him in the face.

Self-helping steps I'm taking

I called Dr.'s P.A. and R. Hallston both today / called hospital to talk with staff yesterday and put big knives away / listened to Jeannie's message and plan to call her / ate supper last night and washed my hair today / went to a movie and decided to increase my medication / picked up my prescriptions tonight. I distracted myself with work on my book yesterday / I did a relaxation exercise today—it helped / asked Jeffrey for a second appointment next week / answered the phone when Dr. Hallston called. I got dressed and I walked to and from the bus / read my e-mail and responded to some of it / ate 1/2 of a potato and some crackers tonight / practiced breathing and I cried for awhile / called and asked Charlie to come over and I wrote about being angry with my stupid psychiatrist

Journal entry-Sunday, February 24th, 2002
This is my "edge" experience this weekend

Shock and loss reverberations, aftershocks / grieving / flashbacks of trauma / boundary violations / isolating / not eating / over identifying with people in nexus / sleeping too much / panic inside—trembling / cut my arm—it helped /

obsessing / being compulsive / want environment in order / hard to concentrate / angry with Drs.' / shame / mad at myself / very hard to reach outward / senses too open to colour and sound / jumping at shadows / want to hide under my bed / empty space in my life now / scared

Journal entry-Monday, February 25th, 2002

When I see these gashes in my arm, I feel shocked and scared. Then embarrassed because I wanted someone at the hospital to see and to know.

Staffing this morning. Four of them and one of me feels intimidating. Their suggestion was that I come in 5 afternoons instead of two, over the next couple of weeks. I'm still mad at both Dr.'s Hallstons for saying I couldn't be "in-patient" right now. I couldn't own up to that with Dr. P.A. Hallston but I was able to say that I was mad about them talking together about me while I waited for the call back.

Sitting in the lounge in the quiet, rocking and being alone, listening to the hum of the ice machine felt very comforting to me. I wished I could just stay there, feel safe and be taken care of. Then I saw the two patients who were in, neither one somebody I would want to relate to and census on the floor is way down I heard last week. So maybe—just maybe Dr.'s Hallston' decision for me was for my higher good.

Tara said today that she thinks their decision was a way to force me to draw on my own resources and struggle my way through this—that the "moving through process" is my growth and learning about my own strengths and capabilities.

Journal entry-Friday, February 26th, 2002

I'm mad at myself for missing group today. Woke up at 12:10 to the van guy ringing my bell. Knew I was playing with fire to take higher dose of medication last night and I did it anyway. I feel ashamed. Called in to Joan who was in a meeting and I ended up talking to Brad, who heard me say, "took too much medication" and he asked me about it. God, it felt good to have him pick up on my self-abuse. He asked me if I felt safe and I sort of lied and said yes—though the idea of overdosing is very appealing to me right now. Not to kill myself, but just to get away from all the turmoil inside, for a little while.

Journal entry-Wednesday, February 27th, 2002

Again, my anger is coming out in my dreams. It occurred to me yesterday that I am a survivor of sexual abuse, physical abuse, verbal abuse, child abuse, infidelity, psychiatric betrayal, and assaults with a gun. The reading I was doing on a healing web site said, "We never get over it. We will always be a survivor of..." No wonder it turns into self-abuse. It's the shame of not being okay!

This with Terri has triggered all my abuse issues. I end up feeling not okay with myself. I realize today that the common denominator is boundary violation. It triggered my first experience of shock when Mom told me on our trip to Green Bay that Dad was having an affair. I was only about eleven years old and it was a betrayal of my trust in both my parents. How could my father hurt my mother that way? How could my mother hurt me so much, by telling me about it? Looking back now, I think that it was emotional incest. My mother was turning to me for love, support, comfort and understanding that she should have been turning to my *father for or at least another adult. I had uncovered some emotional incest before and then forgotten about it. The shock back then on that trip, was in realizing that I couldn't depend on either one of my parents to take care of me.*

Journal entry-Thursday, February 28th, 2002

I am sitting in the lounge on Six West, while my therapy group meets across the hall. I'm locked out of the room because I'm late. I'm late because my Dependable Care Transport van was 25 minutes late picking me up. I am pissed.

Today I wanted to talk about my learned helplessness. Yesterday it all came back up in me, how much fear there is in having something done to me and me not being able to get away or fight back.

I remember that day in my childhood when they tied me up. I think I was about seven. It must have been late afternoon because everyone went home for supper and left me there alone. They were my friends. I couldn't even imagine that they would betray me. I thought it was a game we were playing, harmless. "Let's tie someone up." "Okay, me." I might have even volunteered.

How come I wasn't angry with them as I stood there and it started to get dark and quiet outside—my back between garage wall studs, the door closed and me inside still waiting for them to come back and untie me? I was helpless. Probably my feelings were frozen. When finally my sister Kathy found me, then I cried. Later, after it was all over, I was terrified.

I wonder how early in my life I learned not to fight back? Inez used to say she thought it was when I was only six months old or so, that I stopped crying out for what I wanted because nobody was responding to my needs. Did I turn that anger into shame? Did I think I had no right to want anything? Did I think that I had no right to be here at all, because there was something terribly wrong with me?

I'm starting to realize how I held in my feelings even way back then. In today's art therapy I felt alone and sad.

Journal entry-Friday, March 1st, 2002

I'm feeling exceptionally sad—empty inside, lost, forgotten about and lonely. I feel helpless and hopeless, as if I've backslid. In art therapy I drew my arm and painted three gashes in my arm in dripping red "blood." I printed the words in "blood"—"Don't you get it you stupid asshole? I am hurting!" I was talking to Dr. R. Hallston and then to my father.

Journal entry-Saturday, March 9th, 2002

I'm not liking having the work of, the irritation of and the disappointment of being with Charlie tonight. This is maybe the second or third Saturday night in a row, of me wanting to stay home with me more than make the effort of being in a "couple" situation. I feel like I "should" be with her tomorrow just to give this relationship a chance, but I really don't want to go through with all that.

Right now the winds are howling loudly and I hear the horn of a train off in the distance. Seems like they would be wailing and lonely sounds but I find them comforting to me. I've been working on my book today. First time I've had any interest in it in weeks. Feels so good—like coming home. I did some laundry that I'm going to fold now and put away.

Jeannie called and thanked me for my friendship. So good to hear her agree that she believes we all are healers.

I called Terri this afternoon. First time we talked in three weeks. She cried and said that I was the only one she felt truly loved by. For me it's certainly the same. I am so glad our separation time is ending now.

Journal entry-Wednesday, March 13th, 2002

The crisis is over. I'm not obsessing about my childhood hurts or the trauma situations I've been in as an adult. While my big knives are all still out of sight under the sink and I'm startled to see them there when I reach in for a bag, it's more out of habit I keep them there, than real fear that I'm going to cut myself. The bottle of pills that I sat on top of in my drawing, no longer seduce me with their promise of three days escape into sleep.

I'm here, unafraid, functioning even productively and having an occasional creative spurt. I'm eating and sleeping and taking short walks back and forth to the post office and the grocery store. Last week I did my laundry and that sure felt good—putting on still warm, snugly flannel pajamas that smelled good. The week before this, I broke my self-imposed isolation and called Jeannie. Now in process are plans for a healing ritual with Terri for Sunday afternoon.

I don't know for sure what helped this crisis I put myself through—with such intense reactions to Terri's crisis. I think that a part of my healing was simply allowing myself to be where I was and in that acceptance, it passed.

The decrease in Trazadone which was sedating me way more than I first realized and the increase in Paxil, (sort of overlapping in their chemistry effects)—helped me very much to feel more present in my body, more in control of my thoughts and even have a speck of energy to enjoy things.

Once again I was brought back to the place where my life is more than intense anguish and self-recrimination.

My Greater Power had Its influence in this too, I know. About a week ago I was able to ask for help from a Greater Source. I had totally forgotten that there was a stream of life energy moving around me and within me, that was anything other than my own individual personality that was in such a state of pain.

At some bottom point in the process I remembered Step 3 and the whole healing energy of my recovery program. So I did some reading and I asked for the willingness to begin turning this over and getting myself off of "center stage" in the process. I did a smudging ritual, cleansing the negative self-absorption away. I blessed my house. I sat in the quiet chapel at the hospital and purposefully put my mind on the things that were going well in my life—the little bursts of life energy for which I could be grateful, like the subtle and varied shades of blues and greens in the stained glass window there. I began, with healing graces helping me, to lift myself up.

Journal entry-Tuesday, March 25th, 2002

I can hardly believe that this month is almost over. I had another anxiety response on Saturday, like on Friday but even more intense—probably because I let myself be free to feel what was going on. I didn't have to cope with being in group or taking the van out to my therapy session like I did the day before.

This time I called Terri to see if she could help me figure out what this is and how to help myself through it. Terri thought it was a panic attack—the flight or fight response triggered by something that feels stressful, like I'm being attacked. Since both times I was shaming and blaming myself, I think that one component of this is my own self-talk / thought process saying "...therefore I am not okay," i.e.: me attacking me.

In talking to Dr. P.A. Hallston about this Monday morning at my staffing, she told me it's not a panic attack because both times I reacted to an external stress. She said that it could be an anxiety disorder or it could be a toxic reaction to Paxil being too potent in my system if I was dehydrated and I have been. My dose is rather high and Pail is a tricky drug in this way (used for anxiety and can also cause anxiety when dehydrated, because of slow 1/2 life, leaving the system slowly). So now I'm making sure I'm drinking a lot of water and noticing what kind of reaction I'm having to external stress.

Part of this concern, "Oh no, now I have panic attacks," is that it will happen again. I do not want to be phobic like my mother was, especially agoraphobic. Toni says these stress responses are often the result of feeling shame—not the cause of the shame as it would seem. More like PTSD (Post Traumatic Stress Disorder) we are triggered by something that reminds us of being helpless and shamed and the threat of that causes the flight or fight response. That I've tried to hide that this is happening because I feel so not okay about myself makes it worse, Terri says.

Dr. Hallston kindly reminds me "We're not so young anymore." and says that sometimes these physiological things happen as we age as well, because we're more worn down. This makes sense and I understand better. I'm less scared now.

Journal entry-Saturday, March 30th, 2002

I slept long and wake up rested. I hate this holiday weekend. I'd like to be doing something with my family of origin or with my daughter and Charlie's mom like other years. I like having this time alone today, but I feel lonely.

Just talked with Libby on the phone and we made plans for tomorrow. She's picking me up at 4:00 O'clock and we're going to have a visit and dinner at her house, then go to a meeting together. That will feel really good and I'm looking forward to it.

Talked on the phone with Terri this morning. This would have been the weekend I would have been moving into her house. This is a real big sadness at this time too—the loss of all that possibility for us in sharing more of our lives together. I'm sad with all of the losses in my relationship with my best friend Terri. I wish I could cry. Haven't been able to for weeks.

Journal entry-Wednesday, April 3rd, 2002

I really want to cut myself, have been wanting to for over a week. I'm very, very lonely. I think about getting a kitten, a puppy or being a foster parent for babies.

I'm mad at Dr. R. Hallston. Saw him last night at the coffee shop. Was careful not to let him see me. When Hallston said no to me going into the hospital and the way that he talked about my having cut myself—sarcastic, uncaring, totally detached and unconcerned—refusing me the safety and help that I was looking for—I felt very hurt. I'm still mad about his discounting me when it was so hard to make those calls and reach out for help in the first place.

I have a feeling that if I cut myself now it's going to be really a dangerous cut. I am also thinking, "Well, I'll cut myself just a little, to relieve the pressure of wanting to."

Just called and made my next appointment with Dr. R. Hallston. I'm here with this now, so I may as well take care of it, as it was on my schedule of things to do in April. I'm going to have to tell him I've been angry with and hurt by him.

This is the week before what would have been Mom and Dad's birthday. I'm missing Mom a lot. Want to watch the video of her memorial service and the procession down to the river through the trees. Want to go to both of their family homes and read their part of my story to someone who cares about me.

That I didn't talk about wanting to cut myself in therapy groups yesterday concerns me. Hiding this part of me builds pressure inside to stay secret and to hurt myself further in that darkness and isolation.

Part VII

I just spent 48 hours locked up on 6 West—again. This time I didn't even see it coming and it all happened quickly. I'd played hooky from group the week before Easter. Just so damn sick of all this therapy that only sometimes really fills my needs. Easter weekend was very lonely and I counted the hours till it was over. I missed my mom and dad a lot, their birthdays would have been yesterday. I missed my sisters and brothers, too. Now only two of us left in town. I'd been wanting to cut myself for about two weeks, but was successfully navigating my way through it. I didn't talk about any of these things. Now I see that they were signals that I wish I would have used to begin asking for help.

As it was I went to group on Thursday feeling discouraged. That morning as I took my pills I said to myself, "Another gray day and I'm feeling down. When is this depression going to go away?" By 12:30, as I was going into my group, I realized I was angry and decided to talk about it. My sexual abuse issues had come up big time after watching the special about it on TV the night before. But there were three new people in the group and I didn't feel safe enough to bring up such a sensitive subject. As the hour went on I drifted further and further away. By the second group, art therapy, I was drawing black fences around my space on the paper circle, with guns, knives, pill bottles inside. I announced without feeling, that my plan was to go home and kill myself. People tried to respond with kindness but it was too hard for me to take any of it in.

Fortunately the therapist picked up on my need, asked the nursing director of the outpatient program to talk with me before I left and by 4:30 PM I was signing myself into the in-patient unit. My only concern right then was that one of my daughters had told me if I killed myself, she would too and I believed her. I couldn't inflict that kind of hopelessness on this child that I loved so dearly. I stayed for 48 hours. Within 16, the several doses of anti-psychotic medication had totally lifted me up out of my despair. I no longer wanted to hurt myself. Staff referred to it as a chemical adjustment, a chemical balancing. I was grateful and amazed that my anger turned inward against myself was in fact, that easy to remedy. I did not process my feelings. I did not analyze my thoughts. I did not revisit the past or set goals for the future. I took three doses of a mind altering chemical and in 16 hours I felt well. I was very glad that I had stayed. That decision saved my life.

Journal entry-Thursday, April 4th, 2002

I'm sitting in the small lounge. It's 8:00 PM. I just feel lost. I don't know what to do with myself.

Journal entry-Saturday, April 6th, 2002

Just had a therapy session with Dr. P.A. Hallston here in the hospital. She hit all the nails right on the heads. Shame. Turning my anger inward. These last two weeks of wanting to cut myself not telling anybody anything. The wanting of relief. The illusion of having "power over" by taking some action, cutting myself. This being an illusion of power because I end up feeling embarrassed and filled with shame i.e., powerless.

Now it's easy to see how keeping that secret, keeping the secret about wanting to have an affair and keeping the secrete generally about this sexual abuse stuff in my past—all has to do with shame / powerlessness / keeping myself isolated / hurting myself.

It's making perfect sense to me now, that to be able to go back to a few trusted people at the hospital and talk about having to talk about more of this stuff in order to work it out further, is in my best interest. Me thinking I have it all resolved, wrapped up and put away and that I've done it all alone, isn't helpful, it's anti productive. I can't do this alone and to think that I can is perpetuating all of my old patterns.

Today more of my secrets came up and out and I feel relieved. At least now with Dr. Hallston and the staff here, for the first time I feel almost as open as I've been with Jeffrey, who I'm realizing that I need to see more of.

Journal entry-Tuesday, April 9th, 2002

Today was my first day back at the hospital as an outpatient again. It meant doing all the re-admitting paperwork and luckily, Joan was free to do it with me and I felt like I'd come full circle from her helping me decide to admit myself last Thursday.

It was kinda strange though, it all happened so fast today. I was late, missed group, forgot that I had to do the re-admission process, had my temp, taken, blood pressure and pulse. Because I was late and I forgot about this part, we were rushed and Joan seemed a little annoyed. I started feeling real not okay about myself.

I've got to ask Terri to help me learn more about dissociation. I think that's what was happening. I felt so "not there" and was trying to hide it because I felt in the wrong and real inadequate, so I spoke from a place of feeling very separated from myself. Yes, looking back, I felt scared. But I couldn't admit it, so put up an effort to act all right and don't think I was pulling it off very well. Maybe Joan never knew, but I did. I felt outside myself and it felt false and very uncomfortable.

The only connection I felt present for was when Joanne was telling me that as an outpatient, I needed to be able to come to staff and ask for help if I felt the urge to hurt myself while I was in the program. I had to commit to being willing to do that and that part was hard. I didn't want to agree. I didn't want to have to admit I might be there again and if I was I didn't want to have to ask for help. She pointed out that this was the whole purpose of the therapy program, to help me carry my heavy burden for a little while, to practice the new behaviors that went with asking for help. I really heard her when she told me it wasn't about giving up control, it in fact was about being even more in control because instead of taking self-harming action I'd be taking action to help move myself along in a more positive path.

I wanted to ask her to tell me that four or five more times. I wanted to believe and hang onto those hopeful words, because it still seems so foreign for me. Intellectually I get it, of course. But gut level, the behavior is still so unfamiliar to me. When I am in pain I want everyone else to stay far away. I do not want to open up, to trust, to allow someone near, much less to ask for his or her involvement with me and to be willing to receive that. These are my lessons. Today I start in with this program again.

Part VIII

Journal entry-Monday, October 28th, 2002

It's Monday night. I've been here in the hospital since late Saturday afternoon. I'm wanting the safety of this place right now.

Terri has been missing for eight days and Jill and Dona and I all think she has killed herself. The signs were ignored phone calls, her car gone, mail piled up and notes left behind for us her close ones. Mine simply said "Liz—I'm sorry—I can't do it anymore."

My chin quivers. I'm cold down to my bones. I've been telling the story yesterday to Charlie and Libby, today to my psychiatrist and Joan here, Tara. Sheila listened and talked with me for a long time that first night I came in.

I drew a heart today in occupational therapy. My feelings made bullet holes in it's blackness. Terri, had a gun and I knew about it and I didn't stop her. I tell myself I couldn't have anyway; she could always have gotten another gun.

I feel so angry. When I read her sparse note yesterday, my heart screamed "I hate you". How could she do this to me, to us? Not to even give one of us a clue as to where to find her body feels mean, insensitive, agonizing.

What a selfish act it is—to kill one's self. Terri was only thinking about Terri; how hard her life is, round in a viscous circle with no way out, the extensive physical pain. I understand her desperation, yet I do not accept death as a solution to it. She felt differently.

Journal entry-Wednesday, October 30th, 2002

I just came back from Terri's back yard. I had an outing pass for a few hours and asked Charlie to drive me there. I felt comforted to shuffle through the leaves on her garage walk, touch my hand to the latches on her gates and find the feather I knew she was saving for me that was stuck into an edge of her milk chute. I sat on Terri's picnic table and looked up into the branches of the big tree, the same one that she used to look up at while laying on her back and talking to me on the telephone. The reality sinks in deeper, more naturally now—Terri is dead. The brown shades are pulled down, covering all the windows. The house is empty. Terri is dead.

Journal entry-Thursday, October 31st, 2002

This morning had a staff meeting with P.A. Hallston, Brad and two residents. I'm getting ready to go home tomorrow. It will feel good to be back in my own routine, to have my coffee cup, my chair, and my cat sleeping by my feet at night. I feel scared too. Can I really trust myself not to cut into my arms or overdose just enough to sleep a long and undisturbed sleep? I know now that I will never kill myself, never leave this kind of troubled aftermath behind within the people that I love. It's too awful. It's been almost a week now, that Terri has been dead. I need to keep on saying that to myself, "Terri is dead." "Terri killed herself" is harder to say and to hear.

I left home on Saturday afternoon, wore my warm flannel shirt, black jacket with the pin on it of the witches hat, my long purple scarf wrapped several times around my neck. The sun was shining and the wind blowing as I shuffled through the leaves. Every block I traveled away from my *tempting stash of medication brought me closer to the safety of 6 West at Columbia/St. Mary's.*

My psychiatric admission, a "short stay", has turned into 6 nights and 5 and a half days of trying to find my way through this grieving process; the full range of emotions and almost constant stream of conscious thinking about Terri and her final acts. I've been brought here to this moment of precarious balance.

Dr. P.A. Hallston and the staff listened, encouraged, helped me both to have a sense of control and to turn it over and give it up. I spent my first two nights in the open seclusion room, curled up in a fetal position on a mattress on the floor and the intercom on so I could call out for help in the middle of those long, cold nights. I skipped groups and ate and slept and asked to talk with staff people one on one. I ripped out pictures and words from magazines and made a collage. I called and talked with my therapist. I sat in the chapel and remembered another October 31st, when Terri and I climbed big boulders up the side of Haliakala Crater in Maui. Here, I took a walk to the gift shop filled with the Halloween holiday decorations of today.

At an assessment meeting late into my stay, Jim gave me the feedback that all week he'd watched me using what was offered to me here and coming up with my own inner resources to build success upon success in how I am coping with this sudden loss. He suggested that I could feel confident in my strengths as I went back home the next day. Jeffrey too, that night on the phone, says he thinks I did well to reach out and avail myself of the support of the hospital. He told me it sounded to him like I am being able to draw on my strengths. I step into another new beginning tomorrow. It is a beginning of learning to live my life without my beloved Terri by my side.

Part IX

The first week in February 2003, I was an in-patient on 6 West. My daughter Libby and my partner Charlie had both expressed their worry about me. As much as I wanted to push it away, I knew myself that my isolating, excessive sleeping and missing my therapy appointments were warning signs about the level of my depression. Since going to help sort through things at Terri's house, I hadn't been able to function the way I'd wanted to.

I finally went in to see Jeffrey because I knew I had to if I wanted to break this cycle. It was a very confrontive session. He challenged me on my pattern of pain and suffering and disturbance being so familiar to me that I keep going back for more. He pointed out this vulnerability in me and likened it to an addiction about weak boundaries and an attraction to trauma. Jeffrey told me that I needed to begin taking responsibility for my passive aggression toward all the people who love me right now and whom I am pushing away, including him. He tells me how he and these others feel hurt and mad at being pushed away, scared. He says how they all know I've been going through the hurting loss of Terri and that I've been having a hard time with it, so naturally they are concerned about me.

He asked me about my pills, if I have access to my "stash" and told me to throw them away. He suggested that I do the 5-day outpatient program at the hospital and said my treatment program and his therapeutic directive include staying away from helping with the work at Terri's house. Jeffrey pointed out something very important for me to hear that day, that the thing that seemed most difficult for me to grasp was the concept of surrender and living in a state of serenity, because both are so unfamiliar to me.

The Crazy Quilt

I again was finding it awful to be in that place of no energy, no enthusiasm, no interest, no life. I wanted very much to cry and cry and I couldn't. I wondered if shock treatments would help. I wondered if a change in my medication would help. I thought about calling Dr. Hallston and then thought, "What's the use, she can't help anyway."

It had been five weeks of feeling like that, before I asked to be admitted back into the hospital. I really wanted to feel better but I didn't have the energy to do it on my own. I felt like I had hit bottom. I prayed—sadly always the last resort when all I can do has failed and there is nothing more. In desperation, I turned to my Power Greater.

It always works. The help always comes pouring through and it did again this time. What it takes is for me to surrender my will, my plan, my way, my control and really turn my life over to the care of a deeper, Greater Power. During my hospital stay, Sheila called it the "wise mind", and the process, one of opening to this part of myself—which of course is true, it's nothing outside of or apart from me. But oh, when I get so entrenched in running the show from my rational or emotional mind, it seems a far and long stretch to this Greater Mind. No, actually it seems at those times that there is no Greater Mind at all.

Five days in the hospital, followed up by outpatient therapy four and then three afternoons a week, helped to bring about the internal balance I'd been hoping for. There had been a change in my antidepressant. The receptive listening in my groups and the expression I found in art therapy helped tremendously. I was able to continue experiencing and sharing my feelings about loosing Terri. I was able to get more in touch with my anger.

On one of the last days in art, I made a newly born baby out of salt-dough. The dough had red food coloring hidden inside it and when it started to come through I was scared. I thought that it was blood and I had hurt myself somehow. Then I realized what it was and welcomed the red streaks to symbolize the pain and struggle it takes to get born. My "baby" arrived, symbolically full with potential and innocence and trust and the fragile, beautiful essence of that which I am. Birthing myself again, I affirmed that this is another new beginning.

Part X

Journal entry-Friday, July 11th, 2003

I feel like I want to kill myself. I'm shocked. I'm angry and I feel very helpless. I'm mad at Charlie because we can't be together right now and it's by her decision. I'm mad at Dr. R. Hallston because he said I can't be in his group. He says I'm "too sophisticated" and the group "wouldn't know what to do with me". I feel hurt. I feel rejected. I feel a rage that is big, big, inside of me. I could just cut myself. I mean, I don't have to make a decision tonight to take my life. After all, I'm still hurting because Terri did. I don't want that kind of pain for my children. I need to stay alive to write the book about my life with them. I want to stay alive to see my first book published. Cutting seems to be best. I don't want Libby to know and I'm going to see her next week. I'll cut myself somewhere where it won't show. My ankle? Julie did that and it worked for her. I don't have anything very sharp. I could wait until tomorrow and buy an exacto knife. Saturday night ritual after my work is done...

What inside is hurting so much that I want to go back to hurting myself? I am already hurting. Do I simply want to see it somewhere on my body? In my mind/heart is too much to hold. My heart is aching from when I was a child and no one even knew I was alive. I was so lonely even then and my life has been full of the same kind of loneliness. This inability to be with my lover/partner when I want and feel like I even need that—has just been going on too long. It must be this that is triggering old pain from my childhood. So who do I be mad at? My mother and father are both dead and I've had my time of rages with and about them already. Am I mad at God (what ever that god source is)? I feel young in an immature sort of way. I want to kick and scream. I want to have a temper tantrum.

Would it help to go back into the hospital? To get inside the isolation room and bang my head against the walls and shout and scream and cry all of this out of me? I'm having heartburn. I hate being in this place. I honestly do not know what to do about it. I haven't had a good cry. Tears in my eyes the other night as I fell asleep, but I don't seem to be able to get further than that. Is this the time to pray? It helps to write this. Blessed be...

Journal entry-Sunday, July 13, 2003

I'm in the hospital. I'm not sure that this was a good idea, but then I didn't see it coming the way that it did either, so fast and out of my control. I was really scared when I couldn't get the bleeding to stop. It was just gushing out of my ankle. It didn't take thinking about it too long before I called the ambulance. What I didn't expect was the follow up of the police, as I was being stitched up in the emergency room. They wanted to take me out to the County Hospital Psychiatric Unit, said they had to see me admitted now, since I had talked about harming myself more. I literally begged them to wait for Dr. Hallston's return call, which would hopefully confirm that I could stay here at Columbia Hospital, on 6West. I prayed fervently, for the second time that day, "Please check your page, please call in, please let me stay here!"

I had prayed when I was in the shower yesterday morning. I asked for help from my Power Greater. Yes my relationship with my "god" is more alive now, since taking this "keys" course, but like other times before I wait until all my other options are exhausted, before I pray. I tried to remember how *to do a prayer treatment and I worked the first three steps of the program. Afterward I focused on the work list ahead of me, called Jeffrey and put in a call to Dr. Hallston. Then, there was nothing else to do ... I felt so sad and so mad and so lonely and so very obsessed. I cut myself...*

Journal entry-Monday, July 14, 2003

I saw on the hall calendar today, that there was a full moon on Sunday. It helps explain to me the rising tension that led to my crisis Saturday night. I know beyond a doubt now, that my Power Greater has been guiding and directing me through this. What I wanted from the "keys" classes was a deeper relationship with my "god" (for lack of another word to call this right now) and I feel that connection having been nourished and re-stimulated.

This morning I found out that I am being considered to be a candidate for a new program that has just started last week, here in the intensive outpatient department. This afternoon I was interviewed by Janice Rice, the director of the program. I think that Terri's soul must be hovering nearby, encouraging me on and smiling at the "coincidence" of me working with her old therapist. Janice says that the D.B.T. (Dialectic Behavior Therapy) program is especially good for the treatment of Borderline Personality Disorders. She explained the component parts to me, underscored what a big commitment it would be on my part as well as on the part of the therapist I'd be working with and when everything was agreeable to me, I was invited into the program. I start on Monday morning and I'm so excited. This sounds like a real wonderful opportunity for me to learn new coping skills and operate more from my rational mind than the pressure filled emotional reactions I've been acting out of. I told Janice I'm not even sure what my Borderline Personality Disorder diagnosis really means and she said that the program would start there, with helping me identify the traits that are a problem for me so that I could learn new skills to replace the old behavior with.

I'm very excited to learn more about how to help myself using this small group, and long term approach. I realize that coming into the hospital at this very time, has given me this opportunity. Janice said that they wanted ten people to go through the course and I was the eighth one selected. What makes this even better is that my dear friend Winifred who I re-met in the hospital two years ago, is enrolled in the program as well. That means we can talk about it together, compare notes and maybe frustrations at being in this change-process together. I feel very challenged and very blessed.

Journal entry-Friday, July 18, 2003

I spoke first at the therapy group this morning. I'm getting ready to go home today. I feel real sad that I had to be back here in the hospital after working so hard and having so many successes in my life recently. I feel like I've failed myself. Carmen, the social worker who remembers me from other times, helps to build my confidence. She says to realize that I am making progress, that the times I'm in the hospital are further apart now and that while I'm here my disease is less acute each time. That helps some.

I just want to make it through till Monday when the DBT program starts. It's a challenge to structure my time this weekend so that I do something fun too, not just work around the house. Last weekend was such a disaster. I want to make sure I don't have a repeat of it. I called Charlie and asked for a ride home. Maybe we can stop and have a cup of coffee and visit for awhile. I think it will make my going home a lot easier.

That was a long weekend. On Monday the DBT training began. The Dialectical Behavior Therapy Program is based on the idea that people who have difficulty managing their emotions never learned certain skills or how to apply them. DBT teaches these skills. This includes increasing awareness of thoughts and feelings, improving the ability to tolerate stress and regulating feelings. We learn how to define and achieve our interpersonal goals, build relationships and develop a healthy sense of self. I'm feeling a tremendous surge of new hope. If I can in fact, learn new skills, then there is a good chance that I can keep myself out of this crisis state—all of these hospital admissions in the last few years. The goal of the program is to "create a life worth living" and that is exactly what I want to be doing. I'm excited. I'm off to a new start.

The commitment to the program is intense. First this three week outpatient program that consists of class work each morning, learning the most important of the DBT skills. Then the follow up once-a-week skills training classes in the evening. This six month course is repeated for another six months to total one year. Meantime, participants are encouraged to have a weekly individual therapy session. I am so grateful in that my terrific therapist Jeffery has made a commitment to learning the tools of this program himself, taking part in the weekly ongoing training and case review meetings, so that he can continue to work with me effectively. He will be available for the phone consultations for coaching, as well. There is also a support group being offered, where we can come and talk about the skills that are working for us.

As I learn more about Borderline Personality Disorder I feel more compassion for the struggles I've had in simply keeping my head above water. My life has often been a daily challenge filled with intense emotional pain. I too often have seen myself as undeserving of a life worth living. This new program challenges all of those old and familiar, dearly held beliefs. I am accepting the challenge.

Chapter Five

The Illness, The Healing, The Help

"In the end there is only hope and that too disappears—for when Innana arrived in the underworld, stripped of her powers and pretenses, she was hung on a meat hook to die. In the long, dark night that is the fulcrum of any true experience of initiation, one cannot be assured return. One must be still and wait, without hope.

There comes a point in the arduous journey of initiation, when one finally arrives at some primordial—mythic ground of existence. Initiates often encounter tribal ancestors and helpful and hostile spirits in the course of their journeys. Some sick people and their close relations, have similar experiences." The Alchemy of Illness, Kat Duff

Menial Illness: The Basic Facts

There are many types of mental illness and most of us do not understand them or know how to identify them. The following is a brief description of the most common. This information is gathered from educational material of The Mental Health Association in Milwaukee County, *The Diagnostic and Statistical Manual of Mental Disorders*—3rd edition, American Psychiatric Association and the book *St. John's Wort (Nature's Blues Buster)* by Hyla Cass, MD.

"Affective disorders—These are severe disorders of mood. This refers to severe/major depression and to bi-polar depression (characterized by cycles of major depressive episodes and moods of excitement or mania). Unlike the normal down mood we all experience at times, major depression drags on and becomes more pronounced. During a major depressive episode, a person loses interest in almost all activities, experiences feelings of hopelessness and worthlessness, has thoughts of death and dying and may be suicidal.

Schizophrenic disorders—Usually this large group of disorders is referred to simply as schizophrenia. It is characterized by deterioration in the level of functioning in areas such as work, social relationships and self care. The symptoms are many and varied, though no single one is always present. They include: delusions, hallucinations, thought disorders, loss of self identity, withdrawal and abnormal psychomotor activity. Because other conditions may mimic symptoms of schizophrenia, accurate diagnosis is necessary.

Anxiety disorders—A persistent and irrational fear of a specific object, activity or situation is known as a phobic neurosis. This fear may become severe enough to prevent a person from being involved in normal daily activities. An anxiety neurosis is another type of disorder characterized by recurrent panic attacks and the subsequent fear of helplessness. Persons experiencing sleep disturbances, memory impairment or loss of concentration following a psychologically traumatic event, may be suffering from post-traumatic stress disorder.

Personality disorders—These disorders demonstrate failure of an individual to adjust to socially accepted norms and they are incapable of establishing adequate social relationships. Characteristic of these disorders are rigid patterns in relating, perceiving and thinking. This includes; the antisocial personality (in continuous social or legal trouble), the borderline personality (sudden mood changes, unpredictable actions, unstable relationships) and the paranoid personality (suspicion, envy, stubbornness and believes others have taken advantage of)."

More About Depression

Because the type of mental illness I experience (very definitely episodic throughout the whole of my life) is major depression and because depression is so very often misunderstood and mistreated—I want to assist in educating and supporting anyone who is also experiencing depression in one form or another, in themselves or in someone close to them. I find that it helps very much to understand what it is that is going on and to have some sense of the disease process.

We all have occasional "down" days or "blue" moods. These are a natural part of the rhythm of life and not signs of illness. Depression is not a personality flaw or a sign of personal weakness or a symptom of self indulgence. Depressed people are not lazy or lacking in will power. Changing one's job or school or partner or where one lives, will not truly get at the source of and resolve one's depression. Behaviors such as alcoholism and other drug abuse and addictions only act as a cover for awhile (it is a desperate attempt to self medicate) and then the depression becomes the primary problem once again. Without being treated, symptoms of depression can last for months, years or even a lifetime.

There is some very good information on depression in the book, *St. John's Worthy* Hyla Cass M.D. I bought the book to send to my daughter as a "how to" manual to go with the St. John's Wort I mailed to her and her teenage daughter, my granddaughter. Let's see now—my grandmother, my mother, myself, my daughter, my granddaughter—that's five generations in my family of women who have developed depression. This is shocking to realize, but it is not at all unusual. The same pattern is repeated over and over in many families. The fact that we are trained not to talk about it does not mean that it's not happening.

A reminder here—symptoms can range from very mild (only slightly noticeable to the person themselves, though usually apparent to others who are close) to severely disabling (one can hardly get out of bed to start the day) and life threatening. Symptoms of depression can also run the range from mild to severe in intensity, at different times or in different situations, in the same person. Depression and manic-depression can be (but is not always) extremely difficult to diagnose. The sooner it is treated the better for the person who is suffering it's effects. I suggest that it is always better to err on the side of over reaction and consult with an appropriate medical/mental health professional than to ignore what may be desperate signals that you or someone you love may be seriously ill.

Significant Symptoms

Included here is what Hyla Cass has to say about three significant symptoms:

"Sense of Worthlessness or Guilt—Often depressed people suffer from feelings of inadequacy and self-loathing, despite their accomplishments." Her example—their fear and loneliness, the frightened child inside who has been abused, believes they must have deserved the mistreatment. "People who lack a sense of self worth seem to have an inner critic looking over their shoulder, telling them how stupid, boring, ugly and useless they are. They expect failure and rejection in whatever they do. Depressed people often set impossible standards of performance for themselves. Then when they can not meet these standards, the viscous cycle of negative self worth is reinforced. The cycle can continue to build until it envelopes the depressed individual in a prison of pessimistic thinking."

Sleep Disorders—Depressed individuals frequently have sleep disorders. "The most common, being waking in early morning and not able to get back to sleep." Then there are those depressed individuals who sleep too much, often spending most of the day in bed when they can. Such hypersomnia may be a sign that the depression is advanced and requires professional treatment. However, medical causes should be ruled out first.

Recurrent Thoughts of Death or Suicide Attempts— While most severely depressed people keep their thoughts to themselves until they commit the act, others actually do talk about it to friends and family members. Relatives and friends need to take threats of suicide seriously and not see them as mere attention getting devices. Often a suicidal person needs to be convinced that the desire to die is a temporary state. He or she needs a trusted advisor to say, "Believe me, you can overcome your despair and one day you'll be glad that you didn't give into your impulse to end it all."

Types of Depression

There are several types of depression and they are classified into main groups.

Briefly, I will summarize Cass's descriptions so that you have access to the common guidelines used by professionals and developed and updated by the American Psychiatric Association (as listed in the DSM, *Diagnostic and Statistical Manual*).

"Major Depressive Disorder—a serious depression that interferes with normal functioning. When a depression is this serious (i.e., social isolation, excessive sleeping, disinterest in eating, unkempt appearance, grieving for an unusually long time, overwhelming sadness) professional help is needed."

Dysthymia—a mild to moderate depression. Not as severe and disabling as a major depressive disorder. Life is mostly "just going through the motions" with feelings of hopelessness and low selfesteem. May be able to function at work or school and possibly not even realize they are depressed. In most cases it is chronic, or long term, in nature.

Adjustment Disorder with Depressed Mood—sometimes referred to as reactive depression, results from an identifiable stressor (such as a loss of job, a divorce, a disaster such as earthquake or fire). It impairs the individuals functioning and their relationships. The depression fades with time, generally within six months.

Bipolar Disorder—or manic-depressive illness, involves cycles of depression and elation, or mania. Sometimes the mood switches are dramatic and rapid, but most often they are gradual. When in the depressed cycle, the bipolar person

The Crazy Quilt

can have many or all of the symptoms of a major depression. During the manic cycle, he or she may experience many or all of the symptoms of mania (i.e.; inappropriate periods of elation or irritability, severe insomnia, grandiose notions and poor judgment, increased speech, energy and sexual desire, disconnected and racing thoughts and inappropriate social behavior). A milder form of elation may replace the blatantly manic phase. The person may seem entertaining and fun, even be creative and productive. The depressive part of the cycle, however, can be severe. Bipolar disorder often runs in families.

Seasonal Affective Disorder (SAD)—especially prevalent in countries at the extreme northern and southern latitudes, where there is only an hour or two of sunlight each day during winter months. Sunlight deprivation triggers biochemical changes in the brain resulting in a disturbance in the circadian rhythm, the natural cycles of the body that control sleeping, wakefulness and hormone secretion. (This leads to symptoms such as marked decrease in energy, increased need for sleep and carbohydrate craving). When affected individuals get their required dose of sunlight, they feel energetic and ready to get on with life."

The Diagnostic and Statistical Manual of Mental Disorders (the most current version is identified by a number in the title, such as the DSM-IV) is a guide for clinicians that helps describe and categorize mental disorders. It seems that the words used to communicate symptoms and diagnosis in the DSM and the Mental Health field itself is finally changing—as Dr. Cass says, "to reflect the results of current research and the social/political climate." She adds, "An imbalance in body and brain chemistry can cause many conditions, both mental and physical. Many "serious" depressions turn around fairly quickly when diagnosed according to the underlying deficiency or toxicity. The more we understand the mind-body connection, the easier it is to treat mental disorders." There is hope, in new stigma-free diagnosis and new treatment that is geared to the "whole" person. Finally, there is hope within the system.

I want to note here that it is valuable to be aware of signs of depression, even when you or someone you care about has already been diagnosed with a particular disease and is being treated for it. It is not at all unusual for several illnesses to be active at the same time, (dual diagnosis) such as; diabetes and sleep disorders/high blood pressure and anxiety/arthritis and depression/chronic pain and addiction; etc. Each illness needs to be treated as one part of the whole person and program. Medications need to be carefully coordinated for synergistic effects (working together to become stronger than each alone) and side effects.

Since not all help will be medical in nature, here are two working definitions used in 12 Step Recovery Programs that maybe of use to you in understanding effects, identifying symptoms and communicating with helping professionals.

"Disease—condition of living animal or plant body or one of its parts, that impairs the performance of a vital function: sickness, malady, trouble, a harmful development."

"Addiction—dependency on a substance or activity which causes some degree of harm to or interference with a persons life. The dependency is powered by the tranquilizing (i.e., anxiety masking) effect of the substance or activity." Webster's dictionary

Cause—The Nature/Nurture Debate

As many of us are aware, there have long been two distinctly different schools of thought as to the cause of mental illness. Nature says, basically that, "we are born that way". The idea is that we have inherited a predisposition to be depressed, which is genetic in origin. The cause is a chemical imbalance in the levels of neurotransmitters in the nerve cells of the brain. Understanding this to be a medical problem makes it easier to equate with other illness like diabetes and arthritis. Generally this belief helps one to be relatively free of the sense of social failure and shame.

The other point of view, often in opposition, is Nurture. In this system, who and how we are today has everything to do with reactions to life experiences, especially from the past. Primarily, the family is responsible for the well being of its children and parents are blamed for the child's lack of confidence, sense of safety and ability to trust. Developmental tasks are left incomplete, therefore coping skills are lacking. Current traumatic events add to this storehouse of pain and can trigger old patterns of emotional turmoil.

At this time there is a wealth of new information coming from medical science, psychological and social sciences as well as transpersonal/spiritual disciplines. We are being forced out of our limited ways of thinking. Answers emerge that are no longer black/ white, either/or. What has been separated and divided is being healed as a new approach of inclusion and wholeness is coming into consciousness.

What is a "Nervous Breakdown" Anyway?

In a wonderful book called *Hope and Help For Your Nerves,* Dr. Claire Weekes helps me understand the term that she agrees is mysterious, confusing and sounds ominous.

She explains that the endocrine glands govern and regulate normal functions of the body, in direct reaction to stress. She helps me remember that we have two nervous systems that have pairs of nerves running from them, to muscles and internal organs. One is the Voluntary Nervous system that we control and the other is the Involuntary system, over which we do not have control. These systems respond to our moods. When we are afraid, the pupils dialate, the heart races and the hands sweat. The involuntary nervous system responds with its sympathetic and parasympathetic systems and in sympathy with our mood, triggers our ancient animal defenses against stress, so that we are prepared to take flight or to fight.

The fear impulses in our brains then, have excited and stimulated the body to produce adrenaline and the adrenal glands secrete additional adrenaline into the blood stream to help. Over and over again, these responses in our nervous systems are so intense that the ability to cope with this response, to work with the body signals—is lost. There is a major interruption in the bodies efficient functioning, as a result of emotional and mental fatigue brought on and maintained by stress, mainly by fear. This is what is referred to as "bad nerves" or in the case of intense symptoms, a "nervous breakdown." Dr. Weekes goes on to explain that a cycle is set up when fear causes adrenaline to be released and the nerves produce a set pattern of disturbing sensations. We become afraid of the sensations and caught in a cycle of fear, so we produce more adrenaline until we are lost and confused.

Dr. Weekes explains that we experience this "breakdown" both through the physical symptoms of our anxiety state and in the overwhelming emotions of experiencing many problems, thus feeling sorrow, guilt, tension, indecision, brooding, loss of confidence. In more complicated states of anxiety one may be feeling unreal, in states of personality disintegration, obsession and depression.

She sees the principle of treatment in facing what is going on and accepting it, in being able to float through the disturbance as time passes and one is able to regain equilibrium. She believes that obsession is a manifestation of intense mental fatigue and that in the sudden onset of depression the body is expressing emotional exhaustion. She recommends breaking the cycle by sleeping as much as one can.

In this old-fashioned and soothing approach I find comfort even today, with my broader professional background and more of my own experience, as well as in this scientific age of multiple effective medications that are now available. I wish that I would have found her book in the very frightening first stages of my own isolating and shameful "nervous breakdown" and for that reason I want to replicate her simple explanation of our nervous system and her good, homey, calming common sense.

Sometimes the more we think we know, the less we really understand. "Nervous Breakdowns" in this context, seems to me to be symptomatic of many underlying stressors in a person's living. Therefore an approach to healing that is holistic, that can address a variety of areas of dis-ease with many possibilities that support hope and the work of learning more effective ways to cope with stress, seems to be in order.

Help Is Available

The Surgeon General has reported that as many as one in five Americans are affected by depression in their lifetime and of these, one half do not seek treatment. It seems to me that part of the many reasons for that have to do with lack of education, lack of available treatment and the stigma of shame.

Mental/emotional illnesses can be treated. The medical model of "disease" looks at depression, a serious medical condition, as a chemical imbalance between nerve endings in the brain. There are a variety of medications used by themselves or prescribed together, to bring a person's chemistry back into balance. Psychotherapy is another option, used in conjunction with medication or as treatment on its own. A client will see a therapist regularly, over time, in order to explore thoughts, feelings and behaviors that are limiting as well as learning more effective ways of being. In a healthy therapeutic relationship that feels safe, risks can be taken, new choices made and new experiences successfully built upon.

Appropriate treatment is not always available. In rural communities, access is often a problem. Finances dictate the course and length of treatment. Quality is not yet standardized and most often a good match of personality and skill level in a professional caregiver is simply a matter of chance. Again, because in our society we do not talk openly about mental illness, many people simply do not realize that help is "out there" or know how to go about finding it.

Yet, help is available. I think that it begins with us learning to talk about mental illness and in this case, major depression in particular. To do that, we need to accept that this is a disease that no one is responsible for having and still everyone is responsible for learning about and seeking treatment for. This demands that we come out from hiding behind the terrible stigma of shame that surrounds mental illness in general. It is to this end that I am telling my story.

a slogan that is very catchy:

"Open Your Mind
Mental Illnesses are Brain Disorders
They Affect People All Around Us
They are Treatable"

"May is mental health month, used over the last 50 years by NAMI to educate about the importance of mental health and the reality of mental illness. Mental health is fundamental to overall health and indispensable to personal well-being, family, and interpersonal relationships. People who are mentally ill contribute to the community and to our society in general," according to the National Alliance for the Mentally Ill.

Resources for more information about mental illness include ...

- National Alliance for the Mentally Ill—(NAMI)
- Depression/Awareness, Recognition and Treatment—(D/ART) a program of the National Institute of Mental Health
- Business and Professional Women/USA—(BPW/USA) the leading advocate for working women

- National Depression and Manic Depressive Association—(NDMDA)
- American Psychiatric Association

Combat the Stigma of Mental Illness

"Educate yourself and others about
how common mental illness is,
how many different kinds there are.
Talk about own experience.
Be an active partner in own treatment.
Object to stigma."

—New York Presbyterian Hospital

The Process of Healing

"The root of the word heal is the Anglo-Saxon word *haelen* which means to be or to become whole," says Janet F. Quinn in the book *Healers on Healing*. We are learning that the process of healing and being healthy have to do with "harmony of body-mind-spirit" and she goes on to show us that the word "harmony is a synonym for connection" and that other synonyms for connection and harmony include; "relationship, congruity, unification and unity, order, peace and reconciliation."

"The image that emerges suggests that when we talk about wholeness, we are talking fundamentally about relationship, (which is) the opposite of alienation, isolation, estrangement and fragmentation. Any or all of these can occur at different levels of human existence, with or without our conscious awareness. We can be alienated from our bodies, from our own deepest self, from our closest friends or from society. No matter at what level, when we are alienated or isolated, we are not whole; we are dis-eased. When true healing occurs, relationship is reestablished."

Ms. Quinn poses questions about what facilitates the process of healing and asks about universal principles of healing, saying that the most important aspect, one we can observe, is that "The locus of healing is within." "Healing, no matter what the intervention, is not something that can be given or owned by the practitioners or therapist. All healing, without exception, is self-healing. (The others' skills) may be necessary to remove barriers to self-healing or to stimulate it, but they are not sufficient causes for healing. Healing is a total, orgasmic, synergistic response that must emerge from the individual if recovery and growth are to be accomplished."

Quinn goes on to say that "Today our diseases are increasingly those of the spirit." She believes that "These circumstances are the consequence of a culture in which the feminine principle has been ignored and devalued." She says that we are sadly out of balance and out of right relationship and points out how the feminine principle is deeply concerned with nurturing relationships and that healing work always represents the feminine in action, regardless of what gender the healer is. Quinn suggests that healing in the future must involve major shifts in our thinking about health and illness and that the focus on a health care system must be on facilitating wholeness, which she says, "means facilitating right relationship." She says that what must occur is twofold: "the re-evaluation of the feminine principle and it's ways and the empowerment of individuals and communities to create their own health and healing."

Recovery

It has been my experience over the last 30 years or so that there is a quiet revolution going on at a community level in most every town and city in the nation, as well as internationally. It is sometimes known as "the church in the basement." It is the 12 Step Program of recovery.

My recovery program has most definitely been my mainstay, along with individual therapy and therapy groups along the way. I began my recovery while in search for help with a failing relationship and was led to the Alanon program of ACOA, Adult Children of Alcoholic or other Dysfunctional Families. The focus helped me for the first time to see the patterns that had been handed down to me by my parents, which I unconsciously acted out, because it was all I knew. I was able to take responsibility for learning a healthier way of being. Now working the program of Co-Dependents Anonymous, my new ways of being are directly affecting my ability to be in progressively healthier relationships both with myself and with others. I know a new degree of peace of mind and serenity in my day to day living that I knew nothing about before. For this, I am most grateful to the 12 Step Programs for being there, to my Power Greater for guiding me through the Program and to myself for the hard work of changing that I have done within its framework.

In the book, *Leaving the Enchanted Forest,* the level of work in a program that is spiritual at it's core, is explained. Psychotherapy and specific support groups focus on personality and work with the material generated by the members of the group. "Twelve Step groups are grounded in a set of spiritual principles by which to live." Therapy groups' goals are to help individuals become self-aware and to develop relationship skills. "Twelve Step programs offer their members a set of broad universal values that support and guide them, no matter what situation they encounter." Religious groups are founded on values as well, but require members to share a common understanding of God and certain prescribed behaviors. "Twelve Step groups, on the other hand, encourage individual definitions of God or Higher Power and leave the "how to's" of the spiritual journey to each individual's own way of weaving the Twelve Steps into his or her life."

"Spirituality acknowledges and does homage to the spark of divinity within each of us: it is an approach to life, a point of view, an attitude. It is a surrender to the belief in a greater purpose, a greater plan and wisdom than your own. It is a trust that things will unfold as they must if you just do the footwork, staying attuned to your inner guidance, putting forth the effort, letting go of attachment to the results and believing in Divine Guidance and the choice it offers."

Covington and Beckett continue;—"The spiritual path is a blend of intent and openness to our intuition and unconscious motives, a willingness to trust, a willingness to be tolerant and gentle, and a willingness to keep learning from life's lessons. It is an attainment to what is called for at each moment, on each occasion. Spiritual attainment has less to do with action than with a conscious choice to surrender to the spontaneous unfolding of what is. In short, we construct an entirely new framework for what is useful and what is not useful in our lives, making our decisions accordingly."

The Twelve Promises of Co-Dependents Anonymous

I can experience a miraculous change in my life by working the program of Co-dependents Anonymous. As I make an honest effort to work the Twelve Steps and follow the Twelve Traditions ...

1. I know a new sense of belonging. The feelings of emptiness and loneliness will disappear.
2. I am no longer controlled by my fears. I overcome my fears and act with courage, integrity and dignity.
3. I know a new freedom.
4. I release myself from worry, guilt and regret about my past and present. I am aware enough not to repeat it.
5. I know a new love and acceptance of myself and others. I feel genuinely lovable, loving and loved.
6. I learn to see myself as equal to others. My new and renewed relationships are all with equal partners.
7. I am capable of developing and maintaining healthy and loving relationships. The need to control and manipulate others will disappear as I learn to trust those who are trustworthy.
8. I learn that it is possible for me to mend—to become more loving, intimate and supportive. I have the choice of communicating with my family in a way which is safe for me and respectful of them.
9. I acknowledge that I am a unique and precious creation.
10. I no longer need to rely solely on others to provide my sense of worth.
11. I trust the guidance I receive from my Higher Power and come to believe in my own capabilities.
12. I gradually experience serenity, strength and spiritual growth in my daily life.

—Co-Dependents Anonymous, Inc.

Joan Borsenko, in her book *A Woman's Journey to God (Finding the Feminine Path)* tells us more of the story of Inanna. "She began a descent into the darkness of her psyche, marked by passivity, depression, unabated grief and obsessive guilty rumination.

Inanna, the queen of earth and heaven, goddess of love, receives 14 "me" or blessings of power from Enki, the god of wisdom and waters. These blessings force growth, healing and the transformation that often arranges for our lives to fall apart dramatically so that in discovering and using the "me", the blessing, with which we have been gifted, we can own our true power.

Implicit in this story is a warning. To be blessed is to be challenged. It implies a process of growth and growth often means initiation. The old must die so that room for something new can be created. We are taken to the underworld. Through a process of surrender, during which our souls go into suspended animation and the life seems to leave us, we find that we cannot make the ascent alone. We need friends and helpmates to guard us during this vulnerable time. When we emerge and begin the ascent back out into the world, we own the "me" that were given to us as blessings.

The story of Inanna is an archetype for women's psychospiritual growth. It is a pattern for the heroine's journey that is quite distinct, from the kind of stories that portray the "hero's journey." Her path to wisdom and her divine birthright as the goddess of love is one in which friends are the key components. Without them she would not survive.

Inanna prepares to descend to hell to visit her sister Erishkegal, queen of the underworld. In various versions of the story, translated from tablets discovered as recently as the 1940's, Innanas's descent has different motivations. But Erishkegal fears that she has really come to conquer the underworld, for what else could truly have brought her on such a dangerous journey to the land of the dead?"

Chapter Six

Quilting Pieces

The Stigma

I read an article in last Sunday's paper entitled, "Stigma of Depression Keeps Most Victims Silent." It is now 2003 and I am so sad to be reminded that not a lot of attitudes have changed since 1966. This is precisely what motivated me to write my own story.

Recently I have been thinking about the "hell" I went through early in my life during five years of postpartum depression. That was followed by 25 years of what seemed like constant crisis. Then came another time of hormonal imbalance; menopause, with it's stressful physiological changes (the classic time in our culture for women to "go crazy"). Having thought I successfully navigated that passage years ago, I found myself slipping down into major depression once more. I felt so very discouraged, labeled by the stigma of failure, of doubt, of loss of self.

Then the grieving, giving up of pride and the illusion of control, finally the letting go and surrendering to what is true. This is who and how I am right now, yet this is not all of me. I have come a long way from 1966 and somewhere deep inside me I know that I can go a long way more. But this time I will not hide, quietly accepting the stigma and the shame. This time, my healing is intertwined with the telling of my story.

Tillie Olsen, in her book *Silences,* quotes Virginia Woolf from *Three Guineas,* "What then can be the nature of fear that still makes concealment necessary and reduces our boasted freedom to a farce? Again there are three dots; again they represent a gulf of silence this time, of silence inspired by fear." Woolf says about her own writing, "And here I must step warily, for already I feel the lash upon my shoulder."

Olsen goes on to say, "Literary history and the present are dark with silences: some the silences for years by our acknowledged great; some silences hidden; some the ceasing to publish after one work appears; some the never coming to book form at all. These are not natural silences, that necessary time for renewal, laying fallow, gestation, in the natural cycle of creation. The silences I speak of here are unnatural; the unnatural thwarting of what struggles to come into being, but cannot."

I will not keep silent anymore. I have a lot to say and I am taking the risk of saying it in hopes that I can inspire you to do exactly the same thing. Because we who have known mental illness, in any of it's many forms, can decide to stick together, disagree with how it's always been and brave trusting ourselves enough to take the chance on telling the truth to each other and to those who haven't been there. We then refuse together, to be kept silent anymore. We can find our voices and we can tell our stories loud and clear and we can even learn to do it with pride.

The Shame

I grew up in shame. My parents felt mired in shame for not living up to their parents expectations of them. My mother did not "marry well" like her sisters did; though it looked so right on the outside. My father did not become the prominent physician that he'd been expected to be. We were poor. We were dependent on both my parents' families to assist us in meeting our most basic needs. I think my father's life long depression took a turn for the worse as jobs were scarce and babies were on the way. He was hardly able to hold his head up with both families looking to him to "take care of" Mom in her neurosis and all of us kids.

Shame keeps us in hiding. The beliefs that we are "not okay" because we are not able to function as well as we want to become self-destructive. We lose confidence, energy and even more ability. When we compare ourselves to someone else or someone else's standards for us, we never quite measure up in our own minds. Shame keeps us silent and in that we break our connections with others, sending us back to the dark prison of our isolation.

"We need to watch out for addictive and other compulsive behaviors because those will immerse us in shame" said Melody Beattie in *The Language of Letting Go*. "Shame is an overwhelming negative sense that who we are isn't ok. Shame is a no win situation. We can change our behaviors, but we can't change who we are." She writes about the powerful force that shame is and goes on to say, "Shame is a spell that others put on us to control us, to keep us playing our part in dysfunctional systems. It is a spell many of us have learned to put on ourselves."

Beattie said that being vulnerable to shame makes us vulnerable to being controlled. She explained that, "For many of us shame expands from being the feeling we get when we disappoint someone we love, to a feeling we get when we provoke anyone's disapproval, even a stranger's." She taught us that shame is the trademark of dysfunctional families, and "It's often passed from generation to generation, like a fine piece of porcelain, until it rests on the mantel in our living room." She said, "Shame has its roots in our childhood and its branches in our lives today."

Beattie went on to say that the words are a curse, a spell that was cast on us and it's a spell we learn to cast on ourselves. What begins as externally applied guilt becomes guilt for simply being. Many of us were shamed in our families for healthy behaviors as well, such as expressing our feelings or being creative or having fun or being able to say no and disagree with the "status quo." Unless or until we do something about addressing and healing our deep sense of shame, we are vulnerable to being controlled by others through it. Shame can keep us stuck in familiar behavior, keep us from setting boundaries, and keep us from fully being alive and free. Shame affects every decision that we make in our lives. Today I am learning to be aware of shame as an old habit and as a vulnerability that others can spot and use so that they can be in control.

It can hurt so much to really believe that nothing about us is okay, that we try to protect ourselves by turning shame into other feelings or behaviors we think will be easier to handle like confusion, indifference, rage, obsession with drugs, alcohol, food, sex, love, money, work, fear and panic, the need to control and depression. Beattie says we often don't understand that the pain we're feeling deep inside is the sense of shame we feel for simply being who we are.

For me, I was absolutely mired in shame. At age 23, I totally fell apart. I was having what was known then as a "nervous breakdown." I thought there must be something terribly wrong with me because outwardly, at least, I couldn't find any explanation for what was causing me to be so unhappy. I had everything I always wanted; a home, a husband and children. Yes, I was worn out. But wouldn't anybody be with a new baby, a one-year-old and a three-year-old? Other women did it! My exhaustion simply went with the territory and didn't seem unusual in any way at all. And so my husband wasn't home a lot. That had been going on so long I hardly noticed anymore. Other women went through the same thing, doing it all alone: the babies, the bills, the grocery shopping, cleaning, laundry, etc., etc. This was just the way it was. Yes, I had thought about leaving him a year before, but I changed my mind. There was another baby on the way. My religion did not allow divorce and I had meant those vows so sincerely when I made them.

Of course, there was so very much that I did not understand at the time that I had not learned yet, that I hadn't had experience with. I didn't know then how susceptible I was to social roles and expectations as a wife and mother who was supposed to intuitively know how to do her job (taking care of her family's wants and needs, keeping one step ahead and anticipating them was best) and to do it perfectly. I knew only that I had failed in that somehow, because I did not feel happy. I was supposed to feel happy and fulfilled in these choices I had made for my life. I had failed, though I was not sure why, but I suspected that it was because inherently I was defective as a person.

As previously stated, I had no real sense of myself as a person that was suffering through a Major Depression and in need of ongoing medical treatment in the way of psychotherapy and/or medication. I made the assumption that what I'd been going through in the past was simply related to my disappointments in my marriage and the exhaustion of taking care of three children under four years of age. I did not know how to evaluate my own life as a separate individual outside of my roles as mother/wife/daughter/sister and I was completely unaware that I had my own legitimate wants and needs much less my own responsibility to recognize and to fulfill them.

The social stigma of "having a nervous breakdown" implied defective, weak, primitive, out of control, crazy, someone to be afraid of, put away, hidden, kept secret about. That was in the mid 1960's. Now it is the early 2000's and it's not a whole lot better. Yes, we've had the movies *One Flew Over the Cuckoo's Nest,* etc. and been somewhat educated about mental health and the theory "Nature vs. Nurture." But still, as a society we recoil when someone says the words "mentally ill" in a public place or dares to tell us their own story. We often wish them back into the silence because it is so uncomfortable for us to listen to.

Yet many of us are brave enough to keep coming out. Marie Osmond has come forward with her account of severe depression and talks about her mother's shame that her story of depression too would become part of the public story. Tipper Gore appeared on Oprah Winfry's show and told the story of her clinical depression. She said she wanted to help other people who are experiencing major depression, one fourth of all who are women followed by a high percentage of adolescents. Gore pointed out the genetic predisposition to depression reminding us how whole families are affected. She cautioned about how when we are "in it" we often don't know and talked about learning the warning signs and asking for help using the mental health system. She reminded her audience that major depression is a disease and held out the hope that it often responds well to medication, the biological component of treatment. I felt very inspired by her willingness to say, "This is an illness, this happened to me."

"Our society is not equipped with the ability to deal with the truth," said Margot Adlers' mother in 1965. She was explaining to her daughter, "If you're ever asked if you've been in a psychiatric hospital or seen a psychiatrist, say no." Margot Adler herself said to, "Rise up beyond our past, choose to feel passion and joy." She went on to say that someone had told her, "Work like you don't need the money, dance like no one is looking and love like you've never been hurt." Isn't that great? I have this quote next to my bathroom mirror where I can see it every day.

Poverty

One of the things that I think is often overlooked in assessing the stresses that build to throw an individual off center is the whole area of economics. Having come from a very poor family that came from a very wealthy family, I grew up with mixed messages about money and the status or lack of that automatically comes with it.

In my family we were very proud of our "Blue Book/ blue blood" heritage. The Blue Book was a "who's who" of the local "well to do" families. My maternal grandfather was a prominent businessman who employed "nurses" for his wife and children and routinely had cooks and gardeners working in his beautiful, big home on the river. My paternal grandfather was a well known and respected general practitioner who presided as Chief Of Staff at the hospital and served as personal physician to the Daughters of Charity that ran it. He too, employed a housekeeper/cook, but Arelia was always considered a member of the family. There were wonderful family parties at "the big house" at the lake. The "little house" was a charming cottage that each of his children and their families had use of for several weeks during the summertime.

Mom and Dad had been the rebels in their families and had broken tradition. My father had difficulty finding and keeping a satisfying job. My mother shoveled charcoal briquettes into the furnace at night when the coal company refused to make any more deliveries on credit. I heard stories about Grandpa Rogers leaving boxes of groceries on our front porch. I remember Grandma Casting bringing us oranges and cod liver oil and insisting she buy us good shoes, because she could get then at cost from her shoe factory. We had a charge account at Schusters and Mom and I would take the bus there to buy ring bologna and potato salad to bring home for supper. Mom charged eggs and cottage cheese to the milk man and then wondered how to pay for it the following week. I thought everyone did that.

I went to birthday parties for my Grandma Casting, humiliated to be with my cousins because I was wearing their handed down, fashionable clothing. In our family we'd often be sliding our hands down along the side of our chair cushions to see if any change had fallen out of somebody's pocket. Sometimes with these found quarters and dimes we'd buy vanilla ice cream. Mom would make chocolate sauce for on top and it was always an adventure. The thing is, though, I always knew that everyone in my house felt afraid that there wouldn't be enough money for what we desperately needed and living with that degree of scarcity is a terrifying way to grow up.

The Crazy Quilt

When I heard Barbara Ehrenreich speak, the author of *Nickel and Dimed,* as well as when I read *Tell Them Who I Am,* a research project turned story about the lives of homeless women, by Elliot Liebow, I felt such a sigh of relief. Some of these had been my stories too. Poverty is a learned condition that turns it's desperate neediness into self-hatred and shame. Finally, there were people who could tell the stories of what this kind of loss of self can do to the spirit.

I haven't ever had to live in a shelter, but for two or three years I was homeless and dependent on the goodwill of my children and a few close friends to take me in. I remember in my early fifties, being turned away from someone's home at 9:30 on a Sunday night and walking East Side streets caring a duffel bag of my belongings in my arms and feeling scared. I didn't know where to go and I fell consumed by rejection and shame.

These stories tell about women holding full time jobs that paid so little they were living in their cars and dressing in gas station bathrooms, just to survive. Women who were taking care of other peoples children, cleaning houses, mowing lawns, selling women's' sportswear, wrapping gift packages, serving Mother's Day dinners. The working poor.

Women like me who borrow shoes so they can go to work. Women like me who can't afford clothes on the clearance rack at the discount department store. Women like me who have stood in line to buy food with stamps or wait to be called by number at the food pantry. Women like me who were trying to feed children and pay the rent. I worked part time with children in treatment centers and paid the young and only baby sitter I could get, to be with my children at home.

I was a welfare mother. My daughter was a welfare mother. Her daughter was a welfare mother. We all were the objects of judgment, blame and hostility. The absentee husbands and fathers, who assumed absolutely no financial responsibility, were easily forgotten in everyone's minds but our own. We paid the price and the price was high; constant stress, emotionally, mentally, physically, spiritually. It drained us of our vital energy. It took important parts of us away from our children's right to have us whole.

Loss, Anger and Grieving

It has been my experience, as well as hearing in stories others have shared with me, that there is an essential element of anger in depression. Depression can be thought of as "pressing down the energy." Anger can be frightening in its raw power. One can easily lose a sense of "control over it and many of us, especially women, are taught that "it is not ok to be angry," so it is understandably easier and safer to push it down. One interpretation of suicide is "murderous rage, turned inward." Anger may show itself as anxiety and be difficult to detect, yet chances are very good that it is there. Aphrodite Matsakis, a specialist in Post-Traumatic Stress Disorder, said, "For trauma survivors, anger and grief are intimately related."

Because being "down" is often a response to having suffered a loss of some kind/not having what we wanted, most people who are depressed are also in a process of grieving. Dr. Matsakis goes on to say, "In grieving, you are acknowledging the devastating reality that nothing you can do can resurrect the dead or give you back what you lost. Your anger, no matter how intense, is impotent." Grief work involves several different stages; the initial loss itself, shock, guilt, bargaining, anger, hopelessness and eventually coming to acceptance and going on without the lost person or thing.

Matsakis said that, "In clinical depression, as opposed to normal grieving, there is usually grief over psychological or spiritual loss, such as a loss of innocence, a loss of a belief once held dear or the loss of self-respect. In normal grieving the depression tends to lesson over time, although it may take years. In clinical depression, however, the sadness tends to grow over time. Other components of clinical depression include mixed feelings toward oneself and others and/or active self hatred."

She said, "The relative importance of grief verses anger is not really an issue—it simply varies from one trauma survivor to the next. You may be volcanic in your rage, but have yet to shed a single tear over your losses. Or you may have grieved profoundly, but have yet to confront your rage. Or you may be out of touch with both your grief and your anger along with many of the rest of your feelings. In any case, wherever you are emotionally today is fine. Accepting yourself as you are emotionally is the first step toward moving on."

In our present day society we are not taught to grieve in some of the rich and spiritually healing ways that are and have been a respected tradition in other cultures. We face a void within ourselves and in what little sense of community we do have. Generally, we do not know how to let go, to come to terms with the ending or death of something (parts of ourselves, an idea, a dream, a habit) or someone. Consequently, we are not able to truly honor the joy of the beginning, of co-creating something new, the miracle of new and renewed life, of being born.

The Drama Triangle

The powerlessness of shame not only can grow from, but also can keep us prisoner inside of, the role of victim. I have learned to be helpless and I have cooperated, however unconsciously, with my own victimization. The victim role, however, is not acted out in isolation. Within families, later with "loving" partners who are only too happy to oblige, and even within our systems such as organized religion and the traditional psychiatric institution, others are in collusion with us. The roles they have played to mine, are as either persecutor or rescuer. The persecutor is the "bad guy" like a strict father, a critical lover or unrelenting rule keepers such as prison guards. The rescuer is the "good guy" like a comforting mother, a friend who drops everything when you need her or the idea of a god who will bring us to eternal salvation. We switch roles and others switch their roles with us without warning. It's all done in the name of high drama and pseudo-intimacy. The purpose the roles serve is to manipulate others and our environment, trying to get what we want. None of it feels good. Not any of the role-playing works for long or brings with it any real satisfaction.

That I have become rescuer to my best friend, at this point in my life, after working for years on my own codependency pattern of caretaking, has been a shock to me. My old familiar habit of giving myself up in order to save another, who I love, repeats itself without my conscious knowing. I need to pull back, recognize the child in me, trying so hard to be good and take care of my mother at all costs. I have to establish new boundaries, say "no" more often, so that I am taking better care of myself. It is very hard work. I do it because above all else, I want to be healthy in my relationship with myself as well as with others. These lessons are lifelong opportunities for me to change and to grow

The Rules

Built on lies and deceit with one's self, these roles are extensions of the rules we all learned early on in our families of origin. In the women's groups I facilitate, we go back to these dynamics and see how they play themselves out in ritualistic ways around family traditions like Thanksgiving dinners and celebrating birthdays. The idea is to uncover the unspoken agreements we have pledged ourselves to as children in our families. The three big rules most of us have learned are: "don't tell," "don't trust" and "don't feel." Aslong as we "obey" and fall into alignment, we fit in and are approved of and accepted by the pack. No system likes an idea or an individual who "rocks the boat." For those of us who have risked telling, feeling and daring to trust, most of all in ourselves, we come up against other's anger. We pose a threat and the end result is often being ostracized by the other or "the community" and cast out in isolation and shame.

I continue to find it difficult today to honestly tell other people what is going on inside of me. With the extensive time I've spent in treatment and over these years in therapy, I have found it does get easier. Yet each new therapist or therapeutic situation is a threat to me and I require a lot of time and testing before I am willing to trust. I remember when I was totally out of touch with my feelings and had no idea that I was. My first awakening was to experience that my feelings are not thoughts, they are actual sensations I have in my body. Then learning to recognize and name them came next. I am still in process with learning how to best let the energy of my feeling states serve me, how to make choices as to what I want to do with my feelings. My ability to connect with my anger and allow it to serve me in affirming ways has been and is life saving for me, literally. Recovery meetings, support and therapy groups are filled with brave souls who are relearning to trust, to feel and to tell.

The Challenge of Change

When we don't act with courage and integrity in challenging those old rules and roles, we run from person to activity to thought to feeling to behavior to numb the feeling, to someone or something new, in our quest of release from the hurting inside. This is the root of compulsions and obsessions that structure our lives and take us successfully away from ourselves. I am an addict. It has taken me over 18 years in recovery programs to finally be able to say that. I have used and abused, been dependent on to the point of self-harm and still not stopped using or misusing: caffeine, alcohol, nicotine and prescription drugs. I have been addicted to perfectionism, to control, to over working, to the need to prove myself and to the depravation of food, sleep, money, space, friendship and love. I have used sex when all I really wanted right then was affection and love. I have used people to take care of when all I really wanted was to be taken care of. I have abused myself in anger and despair by cutting into myself with sticks and knives and razor blades. I have tried to kill myself more times than I remember by swallowing down handfuls of pills hoping to end the anguish inside. At first, it sends me way back to where I think that I haven't learned anything. I feel discouraged, disappointed in myself, mad at "god," confused, scared, abandoned and alone. I tend to isolate myself still, want to ward off any more demands on my energy, don't remember how to say no, lock myself up, lick my wounds and try to "figure it out." That almost never works but I still like to think that I have that kind of ability. After awhile, I give up.

The giving up is my salvation. I'll go to a meeting, speak up in a therapy group, call my therapist for an extra session, or call a friend in my support network, (though this is still the most difficult action to take because I'm not sure I deserve the time and attention). My most important move in this surrendering process is to realize again and again that I cannot do my life alone. It begins with swallowing my pride, false and in the way though it is, I have clung to it for lack of anything more substantial in my past. I immediately begin to heal when I admit to myself that I need something, someone and that usually begins with a simple prayer, "I can't do it alone, I know you are here for me, please help."

Reclaiming Wholeness

It seems to me that a holistic approach to treating body, mind, heart and soul as well as sex, sexist systems, sexual orientation, class, economic, race, social issues and addressing spiritual alienation, needs to be the healthy response today. I don't have the answers, but I do have many of the questions and if I can generate some creative thinking on your part, we can continue to bring our energies together to help create new and more effective ways.

I believe that our lives are moving in spiral patterns that wind around and gradually move upward into ever evolving states of consciousness. I believe that from everything there are potential lessons we can learn. I do believe that we attract to us the experiences we can best use, sometimes over and over again in greater or lesser intensity. I believe that we even help to shape the lessons that are uniquely ours to learn. And all of this, I truly do believe, is for our greater good, for our spiritual growth and ability to come to a place of understanding, acceptance and ultimate peace. This life here is our spiritual school. Have I gotten all my lessons yet? Hardly. In fact this very writing of this story is another of my attempts to put some of these puzzle pieces together in a way that not only will I recognize but that may help you to recognize your own particular patterns as well.

The Truth

I've been working a 12 Step recovery program for the last 18 years. I have very seldom mentioned that I have struggled through years and years of Major Depression, Post Traumatic Stress Disorder, Seasonal Affect Disorder, many suicide attempts and years of psychiatric hospitalization. I'd listen to other people's stories about being "in treatment" and wish that I had such acceptable "short hand" to use in talking about my own history. It was "cool" and admirable to be "in treatment" for alcohol and other drug abuse. It was pretty old fashioned, out dated and shameful to have been hospitalized because one was a danger to themselves or others. Drug Abuse was "in." Mental illness was "out." As I relapsed into Major Depression again at this recent stage of my life, I had to start talking about it.

My recovery program, which by now had become a way of life for me, depended on telling the truth (to myself, to my therapists and to my small circle of friends/family that I trusted). I began to talk about feeling down, then depressed, then my struggle again with finding/not finding enough about life/my life, to stay around for. I felt ashamed now. Weak, because I was backsliding. Scared, because finally with a degree, I still couldn't find a job in my field. Ineffective, in supporting myself by my own small business. Dependent, emotionally and financially, as a friend and lover. In the midst of this, bone deep pain and constant aching in most of my body.

I didn't want my children to know. Though they were adults and didn't "need" me like they had in the past, I felt afraid that they would be scared and think that now they had to take care of me. Which is exactly what happened ultimately, enabling me to leave my job and begin to get well, both physically and emotionally. I had no where to turn but to each of them, for help financially. My head reassured me that this was ok, that they wanted to help me and could handle knowing that I was having a hard time. My heart just ached that they had to deal with this at all, now as well as in our past. I felt so "not ok" as a mother. I felt so very ashamed.

Even with the health care providers, I felt ashamed. Having disabling arthritis, fibromyalgia, myofascial pain syndrome and degenerative disk disease was bad enough. They are all very painful, very energy draining chronic illnesses that generally, people know very little about. Who could know; how wrists hurt to grocery shop, fingers ached to turn a key in a lock, knees were worn at the top of the stairs, aching ankles and toes began the day, elbows hurt to pull on clothing—who could know unless they had been there. These conditions are know as "invisible disabilities," which adds fuel to the fire about middle aged women complaining/ just looking for a little attention, the "it's all in your head" response. This is discounting enough.

I was also seeing psychiatrists for medication consults, back on antidepressants like in my past after deciding that I would never go the "drug route" again, (a purist about recovery) and working with psychotherapists on some of the exact same issues I'd thought I worked all through, as well as using NSAID's (non-steroid anti-inflammatory drugs) for pain. I began to feel dependent again on the very system that had drugged me, stripped me of my power, fucked me over (literally) and locked me up behind bars, twenty-five years before. It must be me, I thought, this inadequate, defective self that I am, always have been, always will be, that is falling down on the job of figuring out how to do this life. Shame, shame, shame.

More Herstory

As a student of "social work" in the university system (which I had the good sense to leave as I hit junior status and now needed to struggle through math and a foreign language to earn my Bachelors' degree) and while studying Community Organizing at the technical school (where I earned my Associate degree in Applied Science—Human Services, training as an Alcohol and Drug Counselor), I began to understand the power dynamics of shame. I found out that shame is a tool for controlling behavior. At first shocked with the simple truth of that, and then outraged that people would actually use shame as a tool, a manipulation tactic, I wanted to understand more about human behavior and how shame operates in our larger world.

As a feminist who had "come out" politically, I had begun learning about sex roles and class divisions and race discrimination over the years. My life was my teacher and I was fortunate to be involved with a community of like-minded friends that were social activists who helped pave the way for me to become more finely "in tune" with these oppressive belief systems. That "the personal is political" became my day to day consciousness raising axiom/challenge—from myself to myself as inspired by the challenges of these others around me. It was in the air we breathed and the food we ate, as we churned out "alternative press" newspapers and met in collectives that held true to consensus decision-making policy.

Earlier, in my long hair, long dress, barefoot Hippie days, it was the brave music of Bob Dylan and Joan Biaz and the anti-war demonstrations that brought me home to myself. I was a single mom, a welfare recipient, and a fledgling poet. I thought about things, hard and long. I was opening up and life was, my life was, exciting for the very first time. I worked on a drug hot line as a crisis intervention operator. I found out how much I cared about being a part of helping to find the solutions. Young people gathered in my home at night and we discussed what was going on in the world. We held hands and sat in the candlelight, felt love and felt passion; playing music, smoking dope, making dreams. I had hope.

My spiritual path was taking me to metaphysical explanations of things that made sense to me. There were others, we met in sacred circles and helped eachother to learn how to be, how to make manifest this world peace and purpose we believed in. We prayed. We listened to and intuitively felt the answers to our asking for direction. We understood there was love and there was fear and we took our lessons bravely out into our lives in the world. I discovered my psychic abilities that center on using this sacred energy for healing and as I evolved I realized that I myself was in the process of being healed, in my many wounded places.

Later on, I began to work a 12 Step recovery program. Though abusing alcohol and other drugs had been a problem at various stages of my life, my issues of addiction had much more to do with relationships and the lack of healthy intimacy in my life. I began with a program geared toward children of alcoholic and other dysfunctional parents, whom I quickly learned really meant the whole family. I found out that it had been here, that I learned my childhood lessons about how to be and learned them so well that I repeated them all through my adult life.

I had done an intensive five years of therapy that was based on transactional analysis and called "re-parenting." I learned about family rules and roles for the first time and was able with lots of encouragement, patience and love, to break my symbiotic tie with my mother. Yet it was not until my introduction to Adult Children of Alcoholics, that I was able to see the whole picture; my family of origin as an unhealthy system, on which I was totally dependent, where I learned these patterns that continued to bring me to disappointments and hurtful endings with important others.

After eleven years of working the program, I decided to continue my recovery in Codependents Anonymous, which more pointedly addresses my addiction issues in all my relationships. I honor the traditions of my program and am deeply committed to following this path as one of the primary ways that I come to learn and incorporate into my daily life, the spiritual principles of balance and wholeness. I know that at any time if I lost my solid ground, now so newly acquired, I could slip back down into that dark hole of depression. This is why I work my program today. It keeps me current with myself and accountable to others. Now I can say and really mean it, that "I am a grateful recovering person," too.

I continue to work with my current teacher, in what is proving to be another long stint of psychotherapeutic/ spiritual growth. I am being moved and healed at depths that I could not have imagined touching several years ago. This last week, I saw that he had cut his hair very short, almost head shaved style. I felt afraid at first, of this person that I have been able to build such deep trust with. Had he at some point been a marine? Soon we were laughing and I joked with him about being in orange robes next time! Yes, I am the student, climbing mountain pathways to sit with my teacher and learn, very simply. I take my lessons home with me where they cook for awhile in the stew pot of my soul. Little by little I realize that I am accepting myself, loving myself, appreciating myself just as I am. Gently, I am becoming. What a glorious feast, my life. What joy and beauty, me.

A few weeks ago I volunteered to be the speaker at my CoDA meeting. I wanted to tell some of my recovery story and had a hard time deciding what to choose. Settling on some basic facts about where I've been and how I got here with the help of my Power Greater, I risked talking about: my "nervous breakdown"/ my sense of failure and the pervasive sense of pain I was in/ my many suicide attempts and how angry I would be when I discovered each time that I was still here, and then I told about my five years in and out of psychiatric institutions. Keeping it as brief as I could and highlighting the life changing "re-parenting" therapy I did for five years, that taught me not only that I was "ok" but that I was even lovable and then telling how I learned to love myself, I felt scared. I had broken the taboo, I had told the secret. Would they all reject me now?

No one said a word to me about it that night. That was almost worse because it left me wondering about their reaction. But, working my recovery program, I wanted it to be ok because it was ok inside of me, no matter the approval or rejection from outside of me. Mostly I just felt glad it was over, because it had been hard to take that risk. I decided I'd wait a long time before I did it again.

The next week, some one who was fairly new to this meeting, came up to me quietly and told me, most sincerely, how much she appreciated my being able to talk about what I had. She said that though she wasn't ready to talk about it yet, she had been through some similar experiences and it helped her so much to hear me. I told her how scared I had been and really appreciated her letting me know that my truth telling had been of benefit to her.

A few days ago, talking to an old friend who also comes to my meeting, it came up again. She thanked me for my willingness to talk about my history that night and shared that recently, she went through what we used to call a "nervous breakdown" and now we laughed together about how it's really a "breakthrough". She said how comforting it was to be around other women her age, who knew about that process and what a shattering and life changing experience it can be.

Today I returned a call to another friend in recovery, who told me it, helped her to have me talk about my history of major depression at that meeting. She too, has struggled with depression and the expectations of her role as a woman and her sense of guilt and shame about wanting to say no to a lot of it at this point in her life. In the last few weeks, she's been really down, but she feels better now. My speaking inspired her to start in again, doing loving and caring things for herself.

Earlier today I spent two hours on the phone with my sister Sally, just basically listening and giving her support. She is successfully navigating her way through a "breakdown," with therapy and medication and good self-care. I'm really proud of her. Five years ago, this same type thing sent her into a psychiatric hospital. In fact, it was her daughter and I who brought her in for admission and oh, was that hard, seeing my own sister so vulnerable and scared. This time she's paying attention to the signs, admitting she needs some help early in the crisis, making good decisions about boundaries and her own limitations. She is empowering herself and it's making all the difference in the world. She has built a self she likes and respects and she is not about to abandon herself now.

So, this is why I am writing my story. I want to share my life experiences with mental illness and with good therapy, medication, learning how to take care of myself instead of everybody else and with making some hard choices and changes in my life. I am telling my story, to myself, and realizing how far I've come from that helpless and frail place where I used to be. I am trusting enough to be telling my story to you because I would feel so gratified if some of what I've learned, could be of benefit to you. My deepest wish for our healing is that we all stand tall, without shame and side by side we tell where we have been. Then we get on with our lives and go where we are going, unencumbered.

Chapter Seven

More Quilting Pieces

Suicide

When I orchestrated my leaving so well, did the laundry and kissed each of my children good-bye, I had no idea that my attempted suicide would be unsuccessful. I had planned for my death and I wanted to be dead. Days later I was shocked to realize I was still alive and I was angry about it. I wanted to be dead because I didn't know how to live anymore with the kind of emotional pain I was in.

A suicide occurs in the U.S. every 17 minutes. A suicide attempt, approximately every minute.

Kay Redfield Jamison in her book Night Falls Fast (understanding suicide), said "Depression in the major cause of suicide." She added, "Suicide is a particularly awful way to die; the mental suffering leading up to it is usually prolonged, intense and unpalliated. There is no morphine equivalent to ease the acute pain. The suffering of the suicidal is private and inexpressible, leaving family members and friends with an almost unfathomable kind of loss, as well as guilt."

"We know, for example, a great deal about the underlying conditions that predispose an individual to kill themselves—heredity, severe mental illness, etc. We know too that there are some events or circumstances in life that interact with these predisposing vulnerabilities; romantic failures or upheavals etc. We have much knowledge as well about who commits suicide ... We know too about the methods used; the places; times; and seasons chosen. But we are less certain of why people kill themselves. Psychological states, complex motives and subtle biological differences are difficult enough to ascertain in the living; determining their existence or the role they may play in those who die by suicide, is something else again".

I have had friends who wanted to kill themselves, who believed there was no other way. I have taken suicide intervention phone calls on a "hot line" from anguishing strangers. Yet the way that I know suicide best is by my own experience with it.

I used to tell people that I've made 13 suicide attempts. I'd say it for shock value and in a way I liked the role of "the drama queen." The truth is, I really don't know how many times I've tried. I remember only waking up too often to the taste of charcoal, to tubes being shoved down my throat, or the aftermath in a hospital bed while someone was admonishing me, "Just be glad you are alive." I was never once glad, back then. I always felt like a failure that couldn't even kill herself right. Then I'd start to feel scared, because now I had to live and I had no idea how to keep going.

I remember the desperation like all those days and nights were only yesterday. There was nothing so awful as being trapped in my prison of inner turmoil that continued to deepen into unbearable emotional and mental anguish. I literally did not know how to do one more day, each time. The only solution I could imagine was to stop living in order to stop the pain. I do not believe that anyone can possibly understand the utter despair of wanting to stop being alive, unless they have been there themselves.

Sylvia Plath, in her novel *The Bell Jar,* saw suicide as a romantic and courageous solution to spiritual pain. I must admit I have romanticized the decision as well. I once wrote a paper for a Death and Dying class, about suicide being a viable alternative. I had lost sight of the teacher being a Catholic nun and it took me weeks to finally figure out why she pulled her affection away from me, in spite of the fact that I got an A+ on my paper. It is true still for me that I do not make moral judgments about people who decide to take their own life. Yet I know now, that there is so much more to it than that.

In those times when I was deeply depressed, I had no idea that my ability to think clearly was being profoundly distorted. All I knew was that I thought about all the options and in the end it seemed very matter of fact that killing myself was the only solution. It seemed so rational a decision, so logical. I knew of course, that nobody around me could relate to how I was feeling, so I didn't even try to tell.

At my point of decision making I did feel courageous. Now I had the power back in my own hands and with it came a great sense of relief, a sort of a "sanity" again. I had regained control in a whirlwind that was flinging me wildly against the jagged edges of my darkest self. I had found a way to make it stop. Jillayne Arena, in her insightful book, Step Back from the Exit, (45 reasons to say no to suicide), said, "I like to fantasize that I have everything and everybody under my control. What I really want is the power of a two year old who has learned to say "no" in rhythm with a spoon banging on a highchair."

But I didn't know how to say "no." I didn't know how to ask for what I wanted, either. I wasn't aware that my body and brain were being shot through with chemicals that threw me over the edge into the stress response, "flight." I couldn't take this unbearable suffering anymore, but I had three children who depended on me. What would this do to them? Who would take care of them? Would they ever be able to manage without me? I'd feel shame and self-blame about being "a bad mother." Then I'd realize that I couldn't be a mother at all because I was totally empty. I had nothing more to give.

And I'd be angry, so angry, mostly with myself for all the times I'd let somebody use me, for being so stupid, for being so desperate for love and acceptance from friends, from family, from this husband who gave nothing of himself to me. That brought up anger with my father for never being there for me, for being so caught up in his own inner pain that he didn't even know I was there. I was angry with my mother for her needing me so much, for wanting everything from me. I was angry with both of them for never nurturing me. I was angry with both of them for never teaching me that I was a valuable human being. But I had no idea then, how angry I really was and I had no safe way to unravel it at the time.

I just knew I was feeling an overwhelming amount of pain and that I couldn't live like this anymore. I felt so sad, losing hope of having everything I ever wanted in this world; to love and be loved, to have my children and a home, to have a family. For some reason I didn't understand, I wasn't happy. I thought that there was probably something terribly wrong with me. Maybe I wanted too much. I felt helpless. I felt paralyzed.

Jillayne Arena said, "The toughest lesson for me was learning how to reach out and receive the help and kindness of others. I needed to learn that people can be caring, respectful and trustworthy." This was my hardest lesson, too. I am still learning it. It is very difficult for me to allow others to truly know me. I have a lot of trouble trusting. Yet little by little I do and now I have experience in walking across that bridge that takes me out of my self-protective isolation. There on the other side, or rather midway, I am learning how to receive.

Looking back over my many suicide attempts from this vantage point, I am most grateful that I have survived. In addition, there have been several major medical emergencies in which I was close to death and I have survived those as well. A friend of mine says she heard it suggested in a metaphysics presentation, that we are given several exit points in a lifetime. The soul then has the opportunity to decide if it will leave or if it wants more time here to complete its development. This seems to describe my experience exactly.

Because I stayed, again and again, I am having a most rewarding surprise journey as I explore my life. I am discovering, with a lot of help along the way, that there is a wellspring of beauty, creativity, ability, strength, goodness, wisdom and grace inside of me. I am finding out what it's like to feel in balance, whole and well. I am finding out what it's like to be free to make healthy choices. I'm finding out how deeply satisfied I am when I truly love and accept myself. Best of all, I'm liking myself today.

The Crazy Quilt

Letter To My Daughter

Ginny Lynn,   December 19th, 2001

As I set out to write it is to you that I decide to address this saga, because you are my first born and because you are not here. I will have an easier time being truthful with you in your absence. I write to you, my daughter who I will permit one day to know, but not to have carried the burden of taking care of me. I have spent so much of my energy protecting you three from my pain. Already the guilt and shame for having failed you in your childhood's, now in your adult lives I caution myself against inflicting any more hurt. Yet today I need to tell someone and I am choosing to write though I will not send this letter to you.

I am feeling so damn down. It has been weeks now, three weeks at least, since I can vaguely remember having any energy or feeling any enthusiasm for anything at all. As I stood in front of my bathroom mirror a week or so ago, brushing my hair, I remembered "The sun, oh, the sun is gone, that's what's going on," and it helped me to have a reason for the way I'm feeling. I'd forgotten that every year at this time, sometimes earlier sometimes later, I'm affected by the lack of sunlight. When I discovered about six years ago, that this happened to other people too and was a recognizable syndrome with a name, Seasonal Affective Disorder, I felt some relief.

The treatment is simple, start to use my light box and increase my antidepressant medication. I talked with my Doctor and started that two days ago. I am waiting for relief.

Meanwhile in my forgetting that my body is reacting to the natural world and its seasonal changes, just exactly as all animals and plant bodies do, I am so hard on myself. I make judgments and condemn myself so harshly, as if my mind and will power alone had control over the state of my being, my whole being—body, mind, heart and soul. I've been saying to myself, "See, you can't get along without wallowing in the depths of your depression!! Is it because you need to suffer such agony so frequently? Are you making yourself small because you want to get attention? Is being dependent right now, a way to be taken care of? What is really going on inside that you haven't dealt with yet, that is expressing itself in these symptoms? What is wrong with you that you can't just 'get over this'?"

I want to be saying to myself, gently and with love, "Elizabeth, you have an illness. Your illness is not your fault. An increase in medication should help. The substitute sunlight will help. Asking for more time in the outpatient therapy program is a good idea. You have a right to ask for and receive that kind of focused, therapeutic nurturing. Reaching out is a direct, healthy response. Calling your close friends, going to a meeting last night and committing to being there next week, are good moves. Building in some fun tonight is good for you. Try to be patient with yourself. Help is on the way, because you have taken the necessary steps in getting it. Hang in there girl.

You are doing everything right. Read some Melody Beattie. Eat breakfast. Take a walk. Breathe. Write. Keep praying."

But oh, that is almost an impossible mantra to keep playing through my mind. The other voices, the old ones, the strong ones, want to shout this all down with, "Failure, weak, hopeless, hypocrite, helpless." The inner battle that drains all my energy away, every last drop. I wake up in the morning and mentally say, "Shit, another day," All I want to do is sleep, to be gone from this mental/emotional struggle that saps my life energy, insists on dividing me against myself and takes all my strength and my enthusiasm away.

I feel so flat and just plain dead inside my soul. Wondered last night and again this morning if I wanted to kill myself and the truth is I simply don't have the energy for it. I don't even feel like overtly hurting myself, like I did a month or so ago (and of course never told you). This is just a blah, blah state of being. That's what makes it so incredibly tiresome. This half-numb and half-asleep place just goes on and on and on with no relief. It seems to me that some overt pain that I could feel and grapple with would be a big relief.

Yes, there are things that I'm dealing with now, but nothing new and no big crisis or drama to entertain myself with. I hate that this is holiday time. Not being a practicing Christian and not celebrating Christmas, I feel so left out of the loop and it's a loop I don't even want to be in. Yet the loneliness I often feel is harder this time of year, when families gather and I'm imagining that I'd feel comfort in tradition with my close ones. I have many memories of all of us when you kids were little and now I realize that those were the most fulfilling times for me. I had three of you who needed me and the love back and forth between us was so strong. Wish I could put all of you back in your footed pajamas again and play "Mommy."

What makes this hard too, is that Charlie goes to be with her parents as usual, and I am left behind. I asked if I couldn't just come along as "a friend" who was lonely over the holidays, and she found some reason to say no. This time it is that her dad is too old to have to make conversation and her mom too nervous to have company. For the first time, I'm not mad about how she thinks she has to choose between them and me, I just feel sad. Her being in hiding is no longer even a political/feminist issue with me. I haven't got the energy to argue it out anymore. I just feel hurt. She'll be back, out tenth year anniversary of being together is between Christmas and New Years day, we'll celebrate and go on. I just feel sad and lonely right now and it's hard to get through these holidays.

I miss Grandma too. I hated all those years she went through the holidays in the nursing home, such desperate attempts on the part of the staff at creating a cheerful mood. I hated every time I ever had to walk in there and when it was time to go, how I had to leave her behind. The real times of joy were there for us though when she still lived in her apartment on Olive. I'd always come and help her clean for the holidays and we'd have good visits and she'd read me the letters she'd gotten from an old friend, special relative or a card with the picture of one of the grandchildren's new baby in it.

I'd do her grocery shopping and then always, before I left, we'd make a little Christmas decoration. Often Mom would include a mirrored tray or an antique long stemmed glass, that I'd put a white candle into. The miniature tree was very simple, wooden ornaments like apples and rocking horses. Her festive cards would be next to the tree on a black tray and the golden musical bell from Karen was hung on the front door. There was always the moment when we'd turn off the lights and light the candle, stand back across the room and admire our creativity and feel the magic of our love. We'd laugh at ourselves, at our childlike enjoyment of this ritual and we'd give each other a kiss and a hug.

I really miss the closeness that we had after I left home, was divorced and came back to Milwaukee. I had become my own person over the years and I think she felt relief in my ability to take care of myself on most fronts. She was always my friend, always supported my hopes and creative ideas, and always had time to listen to me. For all she hadn't been able to give in my early years, she was giving herself wholeheartedly to me now. I felt, along with my continuing sense of responsibility to fill her needs, a new respect for her and a mature love for who she was as a person. I began to like my mom, in my late twenties. We were able to have 35 or so years of this kind of friendship between us, for which I am so very grateful.

Sometimes Ginny, I think that I'm turning into just exactly the kind of older woman that she was. Some of her funny quirks have become my own; eating supper late at night after the work is done, loving the quiet and a good drama on TV, enjoying the freedom of living alone, not liking the intrusion of the telephone. Sometimes I feel concerned that I'm too reclusive and might have a bit of agoraphobia myself. I'm extravagant like she was, impractical, super sensitive to other peoples' responses to me, wanting still too often to please. I have Grandma's romantic streak, her flair for poetry and piano chords. I love to harmonize.

My family is very important to me. Being able to share in my children's lives is a joy, yet I am content with having our visits be infrequent as long as they are rich and satisfying when we do share. I wonder about the meaning of life. I know that I have learned some of the secrets of the universe and I cherish the wisdom I have earned. I feel overall, grateful to my god, that I am alive—as Grandma did, even those last bleak and empty years. Grandma always found something to help lift her spirits, something small to be grateful for, something as simple as the warmth of the sun shining in through the window on her hands, interlaced in her lap.

Now my girl, I am beginning to feel so much better. I think that once again I've been able to talk myself through feeling so empty and down, to a place where I can feel the stirrings of gratitude again. Inherited, among all the other things, from my mother. So I close this letter to you and thank you for listening. Oh my far away daughter, I appreciate you so. To know that I can write a letter like this to you and that you will understand and smile here at the end, with me—this is a gift you give to me. I rest now, having found again the gift of my own friendship with me, that this letter to you has directed me to.

Thank you—I love You Ginny,
Mom xoxoxox

Elizabeth Casper Rolfs

Letter To My Sister/Friend

Hey Terri—I got dem blues,

When did we all get so damn healthy (or is it just these "new age" rules?) that we ain't got a right to have a case a Saturday Night Blues? That is what's got me tonight girlfriend, these damn ole blues.

It's the very time I know I "should" call you, call someone but I just don't got it in me to pick up that phone. Maybe I just don't want to hear anybody else's blues, maybe I just want to wallow in mine for awhile.

Hey, this is feelin' just right to me girl. Wallow, wallow and sing dem bad blues. If I had Billy Holiday to listen to tonight, some nice jazz, some Fats Domino, well—that would be all right. There was a time when that was a fine thing to do. I wanna go back there. I wanna sit in dark corners in coffeehouses, jazz clubs and be left alone, to just enjoy my blues.

So I turn on jazz radio and sit here in my little room, talkin' to you. This is how it's been for me, girl friend—just getting my sleepin' down right and then my eatin' gets way off, and I mean way off, like nothin much yet today and it's after 8:00 PM. Then the guilt cuz I just couldn't go to work today. Called up and said "that fall last night when that shelf fell down, just twisted my ankle so bad I gotta sit down all day." Then I went back into that deep slumber only sleepin' pills can bring and got up around 5:00 PM. Now I know that don't cut it with the man at work, but I don't give a damn.

The Crazy Quilt

See sister, I am realizing that I got limitations. That seems so very bad to me that I been in denial. When I saw my Momma and my Poppa in such a slump they couldn't do nothin', I think that I decided way back then that I was never gonna be like them. You know how that goes girl friend. We hate the way they did it and we try our best to be so damn different. But oh, lo and behold, I am finding out I been pushing, pushing way past what this body is telling me (and I know you can relate to that).

I got this thing called arthritis and my aches and pains just drag me down, down but I don't let on. I got this other thing called fibromyalgia and it makes me just worn out all the damn time and when I get touched in some soft place like on my arm or thigh, oh boy do I feel dat pain goin' in way down deep. I just don't get touched much, then that's not too bad, but oh girl, Loretta hears my hurtin' sounds, yes, I can let em come out with her cuz I don't have to prove anything to her, no way. She just takes me like I am. Jeffery takes me like I am too. That man hears about my heart pain and he listens real good and he's helpin' me know just what is really in there girl. I tell you, it is takin' me awhile, but he says that's ok. I am getting' to really feel what's down inside me now girl friend, and it's been one hell of a lot of bullshit, damn denial.

I'm rememberin' when I was little, how afraid I was of everythin'. Then I got real grown up real fast, cuz I could see girl, that my Momma and my Poppa couldn't help me in my life and I had to just do it, all alone. I did it good. But, then I'd get so damn worn out that I'd get sick and lookin back, I think it was a signal, "Hey, I need some help here, somebody please stop and hear me please cuz I just cannot do it any more." But I couldn't tell em in words, cuz they weren't listening to me.

Hey girl friend, jazz is on the radio and I am in my little room. It's kinda dark in here and I got dem blues. This stuff I'm finding out, rips my heart girl. I feel so bad and I feel so alone. And I'm knowin' how I keep it that way cuz then I am home, home with me girl.

I'm knowin' this place inside me best and I am home. Tonight I just wanna feel the good, hurtin' feelin and I just wanna wail dem damn blues. So I'm wailin' to you girl. I'm sittin' with these walls here and I'm wailin' to you. All you gotta do is nod yer head and that's good enuf for me. Cuz I know you been there too, I can let you hear me, down like this tonight.

I cut my eye lid real bad when I was about four. I almost lost my sight. That's been the one thing I been afraid a most. While back this time, I thought I might be going blind, is it coincidence? I had mononucleosis when I was in 5th or 6th grade and I had to stay in bed and get iron shots every week for a year and I had to do one whole grade over cuz I was out so much. When I got my first bleedin' time it was so bad my Daddy had ta carry me to the toilette cuz I couldn't be walkin'. It was at Christmas time. Oh god, I'm just remembering, this is the anniversary day of my Daddy's death. We buried him in a big, snowy cemetery and then we left him there all alone. My heart was broken that day and I don't think that I've ever been the same.

I used to be a weak and fragile child. My sisters said my mama tried to shield me. I tried to take care of everything she needed all her life. Seems like the only way she ever had time for me was when I got sick. I used to stay home from school all day and play with cowboys and Indians in the hills of my blankets and I'd take pictures with my Brownie camera, pretending they were in those mountains. My mother would bring me warm soup for my lunch. I stayed away from school whenever I could. I had the hardest time paying attention. I used to looking out that window at the tree and pretend I lived in it there. I was always afraid they were gonna call on me and I didn't ever know what was goin on.

Oh girl friend—last night I threw up in my bed and at five am. I was soaking sheets in the bathtub, turning my mattress over and making my bed nice again. I been coughing so hard, like I do. This thyroid thing is starting to choke me. I been calling out to my Mamma in bed at night. Just two nights ago, I'm callin out like a real small girl, "Mamma, Mamma, take care a me, Mamma, take care a me." I didn't go to my therapy group on Thursday. I knew on Tuesday I was gonna find some way to get out of it and I did. Know why? This pushing myself to go out 5 or 6 times a week is not good for me.

I am so worn out these days. Everything hurts. I cancel therapy with Loretta because I don't have the money. I call back and reschedule because I'm sinkin' down so damn fast, I need the energy lift.

Don't know if I can keep up at work 'till the end of the month. Some part of me doesn't even care. Dr. Hallston tells me to see Jeffery more often, but I can't, in good conscience, add more to this bill he is being so patient about. I've got to move. It's the only way I can save money and pay off my bills. I'm so much not wanting to live with anybody, these days. Not you, not Charlie, no body around me. I wanna wallow in my misery all by myself, undisturbed by any damn obligation to relate to anybody out side of me.

Oh Sister, it is so good to be getting' down here to this bottom place. I almost have ta be sick to do it, to sluff off this "good girl" thing, this image of "capability." I do not want to go back into all this obligation and expectation, that I put on me. I'm coming out of a long life of denial, my sister. I know you know how that is. I am here in my truth with myself tonight and this is exactly where I want to be. Yesterday, I took my wedding ring to the place where I bought it. They had a sign up, "engraving." I'd been wantin' to have these words put inside and now was time. My own version of "To Thine Own Self be true" = "Be True." I am learnin' how to be more and more true to this aging woman who I am. I am letting these false selves slip away. It's takin' one hell of a lot of courage.

So I let myself know tonight, how much I like being alone, how havin' these blues is a normal thing, how wailin' 'em out to my best girl friend is the right thing to do. I can keep my door shut and my phone off tonight. I'm busy findin' out about me. All is not as it seems to be. I am lonely. My body is crying out in pain. I do not have one hell of a lot of stamina and it takes me a long time to recuperate my energy after I spend it all, so I've got to keep pacing myself and not push so hard.

My body is telling my truth to me. My mind is filled with delusion that I've been living by as if it was life and death. My heart's letting me know it's been the death of me, the death of my spirit, the loss of my life energy. I need to respect that I have needs, for food, for sleep, for exercise and it's a fulltime job to keep it in balance. I take out this hating maybe, this anger with the example my parents set for me, my losses perhaps of the loving care I needed—I take this all out on my poor body. I have cut my arms and my thighs with a knife. This is cruelty girlfriend. I have inflicted more pain on myself than was ever intended. I have not known when to stop, when it was enough, when the price had been finally paid.

God girlfriend, I have really let you in tonight. Hey, this persona, this jazz/blues womyn tonight, is a soothin' thing. I'm glad yer my friend. Ron Cuzner on the radio. Sheets and towels in the dryer. It's 10:00 PM. I'm feelin' lighter now. Some woman is singin' with a perky voice, piano keys tingling. I'm gonna eat a baked potato next. Got my pajamas on. I don't have to keep trying so hard to do better than my Momma and Poppa did. They both felt like failures compared to their successful parents. I don't have to measure my self by my family or my past. So I am weak sometimes. So I can't do it sometimes. So I feel afraid sometimes. So I am just like my parents sometimes. Doesn't mean I am my parents.

That's not all a who I am and I am finding out that to be true to me, even when this is the most frightening, most revealing, most honest place to be— —I am being at my best. Jeffery told me I am being strong. You know girl—strong in the broken places. You know. My past is over and my parents are dead. This can help set me free if I let it. If I move on. Because I have you in my living these days my dear sister, I have the courage to be honest with me. You, Jeffrey, Loretta, Libby and Ginny, Joyce, staff at the Institute, my program, Melody Beattie, Kay Redfield Jamison, Jennifer Lauck, Tillie OLsen, my long time friend Cynthia, Social Security Disability money once a month, a safe place to live where I can be as alone as I want to, these computer keys, my writing—how I love doing my writing, the borrowed keyboard hidden under my bed till I am "good enough" to enjoy picking out piano chords again, my little radio, this Jazz and these Blues.

I heard awhile ago that the blues tradition came out of the people's pride durin' the slavery days. They had to be plantin' those fields, workin' for the man— but they didn't have to do it silently. So beltin' out dem blues, they say how they feelin' and they tell it like it is to dem brothas and sistas. Now you know honey, I aint bein' disrespectful, cuz I one of em myself. Ya girl, I been there with the best of my kin. That's how come my heart jumps up when I hear dem blues again. No sister, Ya can't take dem blues outta a soul, from one time of livin' till de next. Dem blues, feed the spirit girl, and the spirit gets strong.

Blessed Be to you sweet sister,
Liza Jane

Journal entry-January 7th, 2002

I am most grateful today, that this place is here and that I am an important part of it's ebb and flow.

Right now I'm indulging in the absolute quiet of this "chapel," the beautifully wood paneled quiet room hare at Columbia/St. Mary's Hospital, where people come to pray and to breathe in the peacefulness. This morning I really see the shapes and colours in the stainedglass window across the room; calming blues and greens, soft arches and angels. Water, emotion, tears I wish I could cry, release, relief. New grass growing in the sunshine, chlorophyll, health, hope, vitality.

Joan said on the way out of my staffing today, "You look better, you've got a little sparkle in your eye." As hard as it was to be up and getting dressed for this early appointment, I'm glad for my newly acquired ability to discipline myself this way. Back now at this meeting with my psychiatrist, the psychiatrist who is the head of this outpatient program and the nurse/ staffing manager as she read over notes from three weeks ago, I'm much more aware of my gradual process and progress. I'm reminded that I had been struggling to honor my commitment to my part time job in retail sales and counting the days to the end of the holiday season. I had also been slipping down into depression again, my annual Seasonal Affective Disorder now in full swing. That's when I asked for an increase in medication.

God, I am so grateful for the lift I have had because of even this small increment of change. I like knowing my body well enough to feel when I've got too much medication in my system too. After upping the antidepressant by 20 milligrams, I began to notice each blink of my eye, literally and I felt *too charged up to be able to sleep at night without more medication to help with that. So I decreased to using only an additional 10 mgs. and I felt myself starting to level out. It's been about a week or so now that I've been feeling consistently solid and stable, as well as being able to sleep easily at night, so it seems that I've found the best combination of chemical help for now and my doctor is pleased with what's working for me.*

I'm remembering now how very difficult it was for me then, to ask for this increase and for more time in the outpatient program. I was so unsure that my issues were significant enough to warrant that kind of intensity, two full hours of group therapy a day on three days a week. Because I didn't consider myself in crisis, I didn't think it was OK to want so much focused time and attention. The whole experience helped me take a look at how I've been living out of a concept of scarcity, only taking or having enough to get me limping through for a short time. Then I would fall right back into the depleted state of being that I've spent my whole life barely surviving through; not enough time, sleep, food, money, clothing, exercise, personal space, leisure, pleasure, etc. etc. Not enough love. It is what I've been used to.

But with Jeffrey's encouragement, I did risk asking for more therapy time as well as an increase in medication, and the answer was yes to both my requests. Again I'm finding out and practicing knowing what I want and need to ask for, which also involves being responded to in positive ways and being able to take in and receive this therapeutic nurturing. It sounds so simple and basic but it's been a long haul to get here, to believe that I have a right to have needs and to have them be met. I move slowly along. I'm starting to talk more in groups, to focus more on my own day to day progress, to welcome challenges and observations from other group members as well as staff. I'm feeling my right to be here and my ability to take this good in.

Before the therapy group this morning, I stopped down in the Terrace Room for my customary cup of coffee to go. The waitperson greeted me with a smile, handing me the double-cupped coffee, just the way I like it, before I even had to ask. A small thing and it's happened before, but I feel honored by it each time. It's the warmth that says, "You're special here, I know you, I know what you like, I enjoy being of service to you, you belong here just like I do." My heart smiled. I do belong here

How familiar the small side entry way on Maryland Avenue is. This is the way I came in to visit my friend who had AIDS. This is where I came with my best friend during her surgery. This is the way I came in when Sally and I would meet to visit our mom after her stroke. This is where my brother Tom and I met up with her in the emergency room, not knowing if she would live or die. This was the sister hospital to St. Mary's, both of long-standing tradition in the history of doctors and nurses in my family. Walking down the long powder blue and white hallway, past the chapel, the women's room, the gift shop all the way to the elevators off to the left, that staff and we patients use.

Up to 6 West, the in-patient psychiatric unit. Pushing the buzzer on the intercom, "It's Elizabeth." The door being unlocked for me to come in. I'm singing the register at the nurses station, taking off my purple scarf and bulky winter jacket, Bill passes by and says "hi" to me, asks how I'm doing, how the holidays were for me. We laugh together. Brad, who has been a benevolent blessing to me during my time in, says "hi." Joan finds me getting a glass of water for myself and calls me into the staffing room, where I feel confident, *genuine and warm in my greeting today to the two doctors. All three of the staff care and encourage and reassure me that not only do I have a right to this much time in groups, but that it is prescribed in my best interest as my treatment. It's then that I realize again, the scarcity that I've lived with as "normal" for me, taking the least amount, just enough to get by. Dr. W. nods his head. We feel like a team, all four of us, working together.*

I belong here. This is my therapeutic community and I have a place here that is mine, with people who care about me. I belong here and today I am most grateful.

Medication

While the mainstay of my therapy, both in the early days and in the last few years, has been one to one psychotherapy and therapy groups, as well as in-patient treatment—I have also used drugs as an important part of my healing program.

At the beginning, in the late 60's, I was totally ignorant about how drugs could help, harm or interact in me. I'm sure that I was overmedicated in hospital settings back then, when the norm of treatment was to drug heavily to "calm" and subdue patients so that staff would have an easier time "managing" us. I remember being so groggy that I was hardly able to walk. By the early 70's, in my young hippie days, I was working on a drug "hot line" and behind the scenes, I had all the right connections to get good Colombian dope. In the gatherings at my house we played the piano, drums and guitar, had politically motivated heavy discussions and drank a lot of cheap wine. I never gave a thought to my recreational drug use as it related to the medications I was taking because of my psychiatric problems. I do remember mornings when I'd finally wake up, heavily sedated, to my three little ones watching cartoons in their pajamas, dry cereal crunched into the counter tops and kitchen floor. I always felt guilty. I was taking a daily antidepressant, tranquilizer and sleep medications at the time.

I went from there, to finding out that the personal is political and that the psychiatric institutions of "power over" were silencing me. No more therapy now. In my budding feminism I learned to see the word therapist as "the rapist". Of course there were no more drugs, licit and eventually illicit, though it did take me awhile to give up drinking and I smoked cigarettes for a few years after that. I began to learn about health food, stopped eating meat, and baked my own bread. I didn't want to support the mega-markets in our capitalistic structure or take in the life polluting toxins anymore. I began the process of working a 12-step program and was eventually very much against all drug use. Actually a bit fanatical and quite judgmental about it, in my heart of hearts. It was an important part of the times and of my own development.

By the late 80's I was back in school for the third time, determined to earn a college degree. My training at that point was in alcohol and drug counseling. As I learned about treatment centers, how people self medicate to deal with their inner pain, I also learned that drags have a legitimate place in a persons recovery and healing. The issue was no longer so black and white for me and the criteria seemed to be about use, not abuse. As I talked with people in 12 Step programs and with clients in my own private practice, facilitating support groups, I began to hear about successful psychiatric cases where drug therapy played a major role. Of course there are the drug horror stories, but now I was learning about the other side and my mind opened to the use of drugs in a well-balanced course of treatment.

Early in the 90's I had my first relapse in 25 years. My therapist had me see a psychiatrist for an evaluation and when a new type of antidepressant and a drug from the old family of antidepressants that could help with my fibromyalgia were recommended, I was skeptical. I had a consultation with a person in the program who was also a therapist and realized that this approach was healthy drug use and may serve as one of the interventions that could truly help me. I began using medication again and have been incorporating drugs into my therapy for the last ten years. Including my vitamins and arthritis drugs, I take nine medications a day. I don't like the dependency. Fortunately I have insurance that covers the cost. I do like the effects of feeling stable, well and whole with less physical pain. I feel especially grateful for the intervention of a low dose anti-psychotic that is being used as a mood stabilizer and is instrumental in literally saving my life.

Along with the tried and true, there are new medications being developed all the time. Many of these have fewer uncomfortable side effects than before. Of course it takes patience and a good rapport between you and your doctor, as the process of finding what works best is an individual one that requires trial and error. But I want to share the hope of my own experience, that medication used on a regular basis with appropriate medical consultation, can be a significant factor in stabilizing and becoming well. Drug therapy can be and often is the most helpful aspect in treating many symptoms of the disease of mental illness.

Rite of Passage

The menopausal stage in women's lives is important to acknowledge as a rite of passage. Our culture has defined this transitional stage in limiting and discounting terms and many of us grow up with a negative attitude about our "wombanhood" and "the menacing menopause."

While not wanting to support that kind of fear filled attitude, I do believe that my mid-life round of "breakdowns" had something to do with the physiological and perhaps sociological realities that I have been living with. Like the interaction between the physical, mental and emotional self at other passages like adolescence with the onset of menstruation, then through the course of pregnancy, childbirth and possible post partum depression or psychosis—the long lasting cycle of menopause has it's imbalances as well.

Understanding this and accepting the old belief in my life being entirely under my control as a dearly held illusion, I am beginning to set myself free. Now, moving into my older years, I begin to have the wisdom of the "wise old woman" and my living becomes so much more relaxed and at peace.

It's All About Balancing

This afternoon in a phone call to a dear friend, I hear myself say what I've said out loud before: at any moment the earth can be pulled out from under me and I can tumble down, down, down into the dark abyss that is my destruction. I don't want to believe this is true. I want to rest secure in the knowing that all of my hard work, everything I've learned, all the tools and skills and resources I have within and outside of me, are enough to keep me safe, to keep me from falling over the edge.

Yet this is simply not true. I have a mental illness. For me, it takes vigilance every day, sometimes during many points within a day—to be consciously making the choice to not only keep myself alive but to move myself into an ever expanding richness of living. On many days I am successful and the weeks string into months and I write what I am grateful for and notice the intricate qualities of blue in an evening sky. I hold hands in a circle with others as we say the Serenity Prayer. I light a quiet candle at night and listen to lullabies soothing the child in me.

But there are other times when I want to hide in my closet, so no one can hear me and I call the mental health crisis line because I'm so scared and I know the way out is to tell and to ask someone to help and I'm mired in shame for going down, down like this when I know better. I feel only the pain of not being OK as a person. It has taken only one potent boundary violation this time. One intimate other reaching into my secret storehouse of gut wrenching failures and fears, throwing them back at me, then with great urgency getting away.

I stand on the curb with tears streaming down my face. I am 58 years old. There is a full moon. I have been crying off and on for days. I have been struggling with my addiction to a particular prescription drug and to financial depravation. I have not slept enough the night before. I have not eaten all day. I have recently called my therapist and asked for support. It is the anniversary, one year ago to the day, of going back into a psychiatric hospital after 25 years of balancing myself in the outside world. It is almost one year later as well, to being assaulted with a gun for the third time. I want to hide in the small space underneath my desk. I want to swallow all of the medication that I have been stockpiling again. I just want this hurting, this horrible never-ending pain, to be over.

As much as I've learned about being healthy and maintaining my balance, with all that I have incorporated into my daily life about taking good care of and loving myself, with all that I am and value so much that I teach it to others, I can not relax my vigil. I know that I can be knocked off my feet, relapse and spiral down, down, down in an instant. Hitting bottom, loosing any hope and strength I had, feeling only how much I am hurting is a kind of a hell that I visit less often now, but I do go there.

Recovering my balance and learning to live in my center takes vigilance daily and sometimes hourly, sometimes minute by minute; seeing that my basic needs are filled/ continuing to stay out of dangerous situations and toxic relationships/ fighting back of walking away from boundary violations/ remembering that I have thin skin, am protecting myself/ staying connected to my deep roots spiritually/ telling my truth/ asking for help/ being willing to receive it/ staying connected with others who tell their truth/ praying/ resting/ eating/ playing/ laughing/ dancing/ drawing pictures/ making music/ writing poetry/ writing my books/ running my groups/ sharing what I'm learning/ inviting others in/ hoping they see themselves/ recognize something/let go of something/ forgive something/ reach out for something/ keep moving forward and upward in spiral circles and be celebrating their life as I am celebrating my life—just as I am today.

***

As I close, I share these wisdom words:

In *Menopausal Years (The Wise Woman's Way)* Susun S. Weed said, "Soon your voice will merge with my own dear one, chuckles Grandmother Growth. We have journeyed long together through this Change. And now it is completed. You are crowned Crone. What I have shared with you is imprinted in your cells. Do not be surprised when you look in the mirror and see yourself resembling me.

You are no longer a maiden; but always Maiden, filled with blissful, carefree, poetic energies. You are no longer a mother, but ever Mother, abundant with creative, supportive, life-giving energies. You are now, and all the rest of your days you will be, Crone, woman of wholeness, woman of wisdom, she who knows death as well as life, impeccable action as well as spontaneous vitality. And in time, you will be seen as Grandmother to your community and Grandmother Growth to new generations of baby Crones."

And Clarissa Pinkola Estes, from her book *Women Who Run With the Wolves* said, "She must shake out her pelt, strut the old pathways, assert her instinctual knowledge. We can all assert our membership in the ancient scar clan, proudly bear the battle scars of our time, write our secrets on walls, refuse to be ashamed, lead the way through and out.

Let us keep in mind that the best cannot hide. Meditation, education, all the dream analysis, all the knowledge of

God's green acre is of no value if one keeps it all to oneself or one's chosen few. Be the old woman in the rocking chair who rocks the idea until it becomes young again. What you do today influences your matrilineal lines in the future. The daughters of your daughters of your daughters are likely to remember you, and most importantly, follow in your tracks."

AFTERWARD

About The Author

Hello ... I am excited to share this second publishing of my book The Crazy Quilt. It was first published 17 years ago and most of my own healing has taken place since then.

While moving through my mental illness has been uniquely my own journey - the lessons that I take from it, enable me to be understanding and supportive, as you or perhaps someone you love, may be traveling this bumpy road alone.

I am happy to say that these days, as I continue to facilitate women's groups, I am also in training to become certified as a grief coach. My children and close friends will gather around me, as I celebrate turning eighty this fall, my favorite season. It is my joy to again be making my story available to you.

For speaking engagements, book club discussions and interviews contact the Author, griefandgroups@gmail.com

Resources

From *A Woman's Journey to God: Finding the Feminine Path* by Joan Borysenko copyright 1999. Permission requested of Riverhead Books, Penguin Putnam, Inc.

From *The Alchemy of Illness* by Kat Duff, copyright 1993. Permission requested of Harmony Books, a division of Crown Publishers, Inc.

From *Leaving the Enchanted Forest* by Stephanie Covington and Linda Beckett copyright 1988. Permission requested of Harper and Row Publishers, Inc.

From *Silences* by Tillie Olsen copyright 1965, 1972, 1978. Permission requested of Delacorte Press/Seymour Lawrence.

From *Night Falls Fast: Understanding Suicide* by Kay Redfield Jamison copyright 1999. Permission requested of Alfred A. Knopf, a division of Random House, Inc.

From *Hope and Help for Your Nerves* by Claire Weeks copyright 1969. Permission requested of Hawthorn Books, Inc.

From *I Can't Get Over It: a Handbook for Trauma Survivors* by Aphrodite Matsakis copyright 1992. Permission requested of New Harbinger Publications, Inc.

From *Repeat After Me* by Claudia Black copyright 1985. Permission requested of Mac Publishing.

From *Diagnostic Criteria from DSM-III-R* by the American Psychiatric Association copyright 1987. Permission requested of the Division of Publications and Marketing, the American Psychiatric Association.

From *The New American Webster Dictionary* edited by Andrew T. Morehead and Philip D. Morehead copyright 1972. Permission requested of the New American Library, Inc.

From *Healing: the Emergence of Right Relationship* by Janet F. Quinn from Healers On Healing edited by Richard Carlson and Benjamin Shield copyright 1989. Permission requested of Jeremy P. Tarcher, Inc.

From *Another Chance* by Sharon Wegscheider copyright 1981. Permission requested of Science and Behavior Books, Inc.

From *The Language of Letting Go* by Melody Beattie copyright 1990 by the Hazelden Foundation. Permission requested of Harpercollins Publishers.

From *Beyond Codependency* by Melody Beattie copyright 1989 by the Hazelden Foundation. Permission requested of Harpercollins Publishers.

From *St. John's Wort* by Flyla Cass copyright 1998. Permission requested of Avery Publishing Group.

From *Step Back from the Exit: 45 Reasons to Say No to Suicide* by Jillayne Arena copyright 1995. Permission requested of Zebulon Press.

From *The Twelve Promises of Co-dependents Anonymous* by Co-dependents Anonymous copyright 1995. Permission requested of Co-dependents Anonymous.

From *Mental Health and Mental Illness: Basic Facts* by the Mental Health Association in Milwaukee County. Adapted from the U.S. Department of Health and Human Services pamphlet, You Are Not Alone.

From *Menopausal Years—the Wise Woman Way* by Susun S. Weed copyright 1992. Permission requested of Ash Tree Publishing.

From *Women Who Run With the Wolves* by Clarissa Pinkola Estes copyright 1992. Permission requested of Ballantine Books.